Strengthening
the
Family

Calling Christians
to be God's rebuilders
of today's marriages and families.

By Wayne Rickerson

Pastor of Family Life, First Christian Church, Napa, California

STANDARD PUBLISHING
Cincinnati, Ohio   3186

Edited by Theresa Hayes

Library of Congress Cataloging-in-Publication Data

Rickerson, Wayne.
Strengthening the family.

Bibliography: p.
1. Family—Religious life. I. Title.
BV4526.2R536 1987   259   86-23140
ISBN 0-87403-206-7

Contents

INTRODUCTION

In the spring of 1972 at Hume Lake Conference Groups, I was introduced to an idea that was to change the direction of my life forever. At that conference, directors H. Norman Wright and Dr. Norm Wakefield, both professors at Biola College, La Mirada, California, presented a vision of the church ministering to families. I became instantly challenged in an area that I had not heard mentioned in four years of Bible college or two years of seminary. I returned to First Christian Church in Napa where I was Christian education director and launched a family ministry that is still alive and thriving today.

In the early years of the family ministry movement, many people believed that it was all just a fad and would pass away. Now fifteen years later, although slow to penetrate the life of the church, family ministry is having a substantial impact and gaining momentum. I believe that from now to the end of this century and on into the twenty-first century, churches who commit themselves to ministering to family and relational needs will be the dynamic, growing churches.

It should be obvious to all that Christian marriages and families need help. One needs only to look at the overwhelming success of James Dobson's *Focus on the Family* ministry and the thousands of people who still flock to the Bill Gothard seminars to see that people are looking for answers to their family, marriage, and other relational needs. God's Word provides the answers. The Bible is a relational book that shows people how to love God, others, and themselves—which is the real focus of family ministry.

The message of this book is that your church can effectively minister to families. I have no doubt about this. I have seen it happen at First Christian Church in Napa and many other churches where members have committed themselves to this ministry. I believe that this book will help you launch a family ministry that will strengthen marriage and family relationships in a way that will bring glory to God. The non-Christian world needs to see that the message of Christ's love works at home. This living example of the power of God's love will draw many to Him.

—*Wayne Rickerson*

1

WHY CHURCHES MUST MINISTER TO FAMILIES

Toward the end of a recent Bible-school session, our class formed prayer groups. In my group I shared my concern for the growing number of hurting marriages in our class and in our church. One of the women in our group added, "Wayne, I don't know why, but I know many young wives who are becoming disillusioned with their marriages—including myself! Satan must be concentrating his efforts on Christian marriages."

A few days later I received a phone call from a minister in Oregon. The story was the same; "We are alarmed at the increasing number of marital problems our young couples are experiencing. The leadership here wants to do something. Could you come and hold a marriage-enrichment weekend?"

What the young wife in my Bible-school class, the minister in Oregon, myself, and thousands of other concerned Christians like you are observing, is the cumulative affects of the world's pressure on the Christian home. What's happening to Christian marriages and families is not sudden nor is it

What's happening to Christian marriages is not a surprise.

It is the result of a cancer that has been weakening us for years.

a surprise. We are now seeing clearly the cancer that has been weakening families and marriages for years—and it's not a pretty sight. With almost one out of every two marriages ending in divorce, and the divorce rate increasing within the church, few have to be convinced that the Christian family is under attack. We need to be equally convinced, however, that the church can and must develop ministries to help strengthen the Christian home.

The Pressure to Conform

The world's view of family and marriage is having an effect on the Christian home. What the world has to say about the home is often in direct opposition to the Biblical view. Let's take a look at some of the differences.

World View of Love and Marriage	Biblical View of Love and Marriage
1. Love is a feeling. "When the feeling is gone, so is love."	1. Love is a decision, it is action and a commitment. (1 Corinthians 13; John 15:12, 13)
2. Love is conditional. "I will love you if you meet my needs."	2. Love is unconditional, not based on your performance. (1 John 4:7-11)
3. Marriage can be temporary. "If I am unhappy, I can divorce."	3. Marriage is permanent, a covenant between you two and God. (Genesis 2:24; Matthew 19:3-6)

We are bombarded by the world's subtle and not so subtle messages from advertisements, literature, music, television, movies, education, friends, neighbors, and business associates. And some of us are listening—there is a definite conforming of some Christian marriages to the world's thoughts, attitudes, and actions.

The Power to Be Transformed

The pressure to be conformed to the world's standards is not new. Jesus was aware of the danger and prayed that His disciples would be able to withstand the pressures of the world. "I do not ask Thee to take them out of the world, but to keep them from the evil one . . . sanctify them in the truth; Thy word is truth" (John 17:15, 17).

We are in the world. We cannot isolate our marriages and families from evil messages but we do have available to us the power to have Godly marriages and families. To plug into this power, we must listen to the truth and apply it to our lives. There must be a continual renewing of our minds with the truth— the Biblical standards for our marriage and families. Paul says, "And do not be conformed to this world, but be transformed by the renewing of your mind, that you may prove what the will of God is, that which is good and acceptable and perfect" (Romans 12:2).

We are in the world. We cannot isolate our families. But we do have the power available to us to be transformed.

The "good and acceptable and perfect" will of God for our marriages and our families comes when we study His word and apply it to our lives.

A Heart for Families

Do you have a heart for families? I assume that you do because you are reading this book. You are a part of a growing number of Christians who feel grief over what is happening to families. Your heart is broken when you think of the crumbling marriages and families in our churches. You have that same kind of grief that Nehemiah had when he heard of the crumbling wall of Jerusalem that symbolized the deterioration of that nation. Listen to Nehemiah, "And they said to me, 'The remnant there in the province who survived the captivity are in great distress and reproach, and the wall of Jerusalem is broken down and its gates are burned with fire.' Now it came about when I heard these words, I sat down and wept and mourned for days; and I was fasting and praying before the God of heaven (Nehemiah 1:3, 4).

For marriages and families to be nurtured and rebuilt, our church leaders must first, like Nehemiah, have broken hearts over what is happening. Change is going to require some fasting and praying. Only this kind of compassion will move our churches to dynamic ministries to families. As things stand now, a very small percentage of churches have any kind of specific and consistent ministry to families. My observation is less than one percent have what I would call family ministries.

For churches to build stronger families (preventive medicine) and rebuild families (curative medicine), there must be a planned approach that includes specific helps. I believe that this is a must—not an option. I know that is a strong statement, and I want to make an even stronger one.

I believe that a church who doesn't have a specific ministry to families is failing its families and contributing to the breakdown of families in our society.

A Relational Ministry

A ministry to families deals primarily with relationships. This relational ministry is deeply rooted in the central doctrine of the Bible. That central doctrine is that God loves us so much that he sent His Son to live and die so that we can have a loving relationship with Him and others. Jesus made this clear when the lawyer asked Him which was the greatest commandment. Jesus answered, ". . . 'You shall love the Lord your God with all your heart, and with all your soul, and with all your mind.' This is the great and foremost commandment. And a second is like it, 'You shall love your neighbor as yourself.' On these two commandments depend the whole Law and the Prophets" (Matthew 22:37-39).

The focus of the entire Bible is on these three loves: love of God, love of others, and love of self (implied). Jesus came to show us how to love God and how that love would affect our love toward others and ourself. Family ministry takes this topic of love and helps people apply it to their family relationships. The overall goal of family ministry is the same goal that Paul had for the early church. He told Timothy, "The goal of our instruction is love from a pure heart and a good conscience and a sincere faith" (1 Timothy 1:5).

> *The focus of the entire Bible is on the love of God, the love of others, and the love of ourselves.*

A Relational Ministry for a Relational Society

Human relationships have never been in greater need of help in the history of the world. The expectations for relationships today are enormous. Historically, the family has been so busy surviving that it had neither the time nor the energy to devote to building quality relationships. We have the time today, the need has never been greater, and we must devote the energy.

Dolores Curran in her book, *Traits of a Healthy Family*, lists the five historical functions of the family. They are: 1) to achieve economic survival, 2) to provide protection, 3) to pass on the religious faith, 4) to educate its young, and

5) to confer status. Curran adds a new function of the current family, 6) to build better relationships.[1] Curran is not saying that the historical family was not relational, but she is emphasizing that there was so much effort put into feeding, protecting, and educating a family, that there was not a lot of time and energy left for concentrating on relationships.

In our current society, the amount of time and energy spent on the five historic functions of the family is dramatically less. That gives us more of our personal resources to spend on relationships. That is why we have seen a proliferation of books on the family, communication, and human potential in the last fifteen years. While there are many family resources, both Christian and secular, the number of people taking advantage of these helps is relatively small. The need remains enormous in helping people acquire the relational *attitudes* and *skills* to live the abundant life that God has made available to us. The church has the potential to help people meet these relational needs. We can help people apply God's word to their lives and learn to love one another.

I believe that the dynamic churches of the eighties and nineties will be the churches that give practical training in relational attitudes and skills.

---

[1] Dolores Curran, *Traits of a Healthy Family* (Minneapolis: Winston Press, Inc., 1983), pp 4, 5, 10.

Training for Abundant Relationships

The task of family ministry is to teach people how to experience abundant relationships within their families. By abundant relationships I do not mean problem-free relationships. All marriages and families are going to experience problems and suffering at some time. However, to endure damaged relationships a majority of the time is not God's will. The abundant family and marriage relationship is one where persons experience a warm intimate relationship while realizing there will be some conflict and pain because we are all imperfect. The answer is for the church to offer teaching that will help shape attitudes and build skills.

Attitudes are shaped by what we believe. As Christians, our attitudes should be based on God's revealed truth—His precepts. God's precepts produce Biblical attitudes and heart responses. For example, God's Word says that marriage is to be permanent. If we believe that, then our attitude will be, "I will do whatever I need to, to make this marriage work." God's precepts are the bottom line of family ministries. They are absolute.

God's precepts never change. His Word is the foundation of family ministry.

A couple might accept God's precepts on marriage, have a Biblical attitude, but still not be doing well in their marriage. They might not have the necessary skills to live abundantly. This brings us to another task of family ministries; helping people develop the necessary skills for intimate relationships within the family. This involves *discovered truth* or *concepts.* Discovered truth is what man has discovered about himself and the universe. God's precepts and man's concepts must work together in order for relationships to be successful. Let's look at a couple who accept God's precepts on marriage, have a Biblical attitude, but still have ongoing pain in their marriage. The problem may be that they have never learned how to communicate how they feel or specifically what they need from the other person in the marriage. They need to learn some communication concepts or skills. They need to learn to express how they feel in a loving way and to ask for what they want from each other. These are communication skills that can be taught. Communication is a discovered truth and helps apply God's Word to daily life.

Precepts and Concepts

Revealed Truth   Discovered Truth

| Biblical Precepts | Concepts |

Produce   Produce

| Biblical Attitudes (Heart Response) | Relational Skills |

God's precepts never change. His Word is the foundation of family ministry and always comes first. Discovered truth, or concepts, are what we think we have discovered about how God has made man and the universe. Medicine, for example, is constantly discovering more about how the body works and what can be done to heal it. That is discovered truth. In family ministry, discovered truth is even more subjective. It is about interpersonal relations and includes such things as communication skills, training in methods of child discipline, and how to manage emotions. We should never treat these concepts as revealed truth. These are simply concepts that we have found to be accurate and helpful in helping people live out God's precepts. These concepts should always support God's precepts and never contradict them.

Your Church Can Minister to Families

I believe that your church body can develop a significant ministry to families. It is my conviction that family ministries are God's will, and what God expects, God enables. I have been involved in family ministries at First Christian Church in Napa, California for more than nine years. We started on a small scale with a vision and little else. Over a period of years, we have developed our ministry to meet more family needs and have seen significant success.

In a recent church survey, ninety-seven percent of the church responded that family ministries were helping people in our church, and more than fifty percent had been personally helped by family ministries. At this point, more than ten percent of our budget goes directly to helping families. This includes a family ministry staff salary, support staff to family ministries, and programming.

Any size church body can minister to families. Whether you are a layman, elder, or minister, you can be the catalyst. Just one person with the concern and the vision to develop a significant family ministry can bring one into being. Five years ago, a lay couple in a church in Oregon heard about our ministry to families and asked if they could come to one of our marriage retreats. They attended our retreat, returned to their church, and helped plan their own marriage retreat. Over the last five years I have watched this couple develop a wonderful ministry to families in that church. *You can do the same in your church!* The purpose of this book is to give you the tools you need to meet the needs of families in your church.

It should be obvious to all that Christian marriages and families need help.

You, and your church, can provide this help.

DISCUSSION QUESTIONS

1. What indication is there in your church body that marriages and families are being influenced by the pressure to conform to the world's standards?

2. Do you have a heart for families? Write down some of your *thoughts* and *feelings* about the need to minister to families in your church.

3. Why, in your opinion, do such a small percentage of churches have specific ministries to families?

4. What do you think about the author's statement, "I believe that a church that does not have a specific ministry to families is failing its families and contributing to the breakdown of families in our society"?

5. What do you think and how do you feel about the author's statement that a relational ministry is the central doctrine of the Bible?

6. The author makes a distinction between precepts and concepts saying that both are important parts of a family ministry. Do you agree or disagree? Why or why not?

7. The author says that it is important for a church body to provide an atmosphere in which people can share marriage and family problems. How does your church rate in this area?

low   medium   high
1 2 3 4 5 6 7 8 9 10

8. Will you be the catalyst for family ministries in your church? Explain.

2

PLANNING YOUR FAMILY MINISTRY

You can make the difference! You can
be the catalyst God uses to restore families to the units of strength and support
that He intended them to be. God has
always used individuals to rebuild His
ideals. We read in the previous chapter
how God used Nehemiah to rebuild the
walls of Jerusalem. Nehemiah followed
a logical, planned procedure for the
monumental task, and you can follow
his procedure to launch a successful
family ministry.

*You __can__
make the
difference!*

Personal Preparation

Nehemiah first *saw* the need, *felt* the
need, *prepared himself* to do God's will,
and then accepted responsibility for the
work to be done.

1. **Pay Attention to the Facts**
   (Nehemiah 1:2, 3)

Nehemiah listened to the facts when his brother and associates told about the conditions of the wall of Jerusalem. It is essential that we pay attention to the facts about families in our nation and in our churches. What's happening to your families? What are their needs?

2. Respond to Facts with Grief (Nehemiah 1:4a)

Nehemiah wept and mourned for days. Our hearts should be broken over the broken families in our church and nation. Do you have a burden for them?

3. Pray and Fast (Nehemiah 1:4b)

Nehemiah's grief moved him to a period of fasting and prayer to God on behalf of Israel. We need to be equally as concerned for our families. Are you praying for marriages and families in your church? Have you ever fasted on their behalf? Is your church leadership praying diligently for families?

Someone must take personal responsibility to become God's rebuilder of families.

4. Take Personal Responsibility (Nehemiah 1:5-11)

In his prayer, Nehemiah took personal responsibility for his part in not keeping the statutes, commandments, and ordinances of God. Nehemiah repented and then asked God to listen to him and other faithful people who were praying for his success in asking the king's permission to rebuild the wall. Nehemiah took personal responsibility to become God's rebuilder.

To meet the needs of families in the

church, someone must take personal responsibility to become God's rebuilder of families. Are you willing to be that person? Do you have others praying with you about family ministries?

Implementing the Plan

The rest of Nehemiah's logical steps for rebuilding the wall involved putting his plan into action. He was careful to follow proper procedures in order to reach his goal, and we would be wise to follow his example. Nehemiah's proper procedures included:

5. Asking Permission
6. Assessing the Needs
7. Building a Team
8. Planning to Build
9. Overcoming the Opposition

Chapter nine will cover these steps in detail, but first you will want to examine the need for a family ministry, and the very practical help that such a ministry can provide.

Who Benefits
From Family Ministries?

As the title "Family Ministries" indicates, those primarily benefiting from the ministries are families. By families I mean married couples, married couples with children, and single-parent families. It is obvious that the definition of "family" in our society is changing. According to the Census Bureau, "The traditional model of the typical American family, in which the father goes to work earning the bread and mother stays home rearing the children, no longer conforms to reality. Of today's sixty-two million American families," the Census Bureau declares, "only 9.4 million (or fifteen percent) fit the old-fashioned stereotype. The facts are that in almost twenty-two percent of the nation's families, both parents are wage earners; in eleven percent, there is only one parent; the remaining families have no children in the home."[2]

Five Purposes of a Family Ministry

An effective family ministry has five main purposes, or goals. These purposes are:

1. To Encourage
a Vital Relationship With God
Those who attempt to minister must never forget that real growth comes through applying the Word and maintaining a personal relationship with God. Whatever we do must encourage persons to have a vital relationship with God.

2. To Strengthen
Husband and Wife Relationships
Other than encouraging a vital relationship with God, strengthening husband and wife relationships is the highest priority in family ministries. One of

the church's greatest responsibilities is to provide encouragement and training to strengthen marriage relationships.

3. To Build Family Strengths

There are attitudes and skills that families must develop in order to be healthy. Knowing how to spend time together, developing traditions, and communicating are a few of these skills. Couples and single parents need to know effective ways to discipline their children. There are many other family strengths that need to be learned.

4. To Enable Parents to Teach Christian Values

God has given parents the *primary* responsibility of teaching Christian values to their children. The church needs to provide training and resources to enable parents to fulfill this responsibility.

5. To Develop Relational Strengths

All of us need to continually develop our abilities to relate to one another. We can always learn how to love God, ourselves, and others in a more effective way. Workshops that teach how to manage anger, confront in love, manage stress, deal with mid-life crises, and prepare for retirement are examples of how family ministries can help people build relational strengths.

Family ministries should result in families and marriages that glorify God and minister to others.

DISCUSSION QUESTIONS

1. Which step in Nehemiah's personal preparation will be the most important for you in establishing a family ministry?

2. How many different types of families are there in your congregation? How many of them could benefit from a family ministry?

3. Which of the five purposes for a family ministry is most important for your church to focus on?

STRENGTHENING
MARRIAGE RELATIONSHIPS

What's Happening
to Christian Marriages Today?

In chapter one, I touched on some issues threatening Christian marriages today. In this chapter, we will review these briefly and look at other areas that are contributing to the breakdown of marriages in the church.

1. Loss of Biblical Framework

Without a Biblical framework for love and marriage, Christian marriages will quickly get into trouble and stay in trouble. Too many couples have adopted a worldly view of love and marriage. While I know of no divorce statistics on Christian couples, the concensus of the family specialists I know is that the divorce rate among Christians is growing at an alarming speed. Most believe that we are rapidly catching up to the general population divorce rate. While the divorce rate has declined slightly in the last few years, still almost one out of two people getting married today will divorce. Divorced persons represent nine percent of the population, up from four percent in 1970.[3]

Too many couples have adopted a worldly view of love and marriage.

---

[3]*USA Today Newspaper*, September 16, 1985

2. Focus on the Individual

In direct contrast to Christ's admonition to become servants and meet the needs of others, people in our country have become obsessed by their own needs. As a *U.S. News and World Report* feature on the family stated, "There is a lack of family cohesion now, a product of the celebration of the individual."[4] With each family member focusing on himself, there is little hope for family cohesion or intimate marriages.

3. Parallel Marriages

Closely associated with the "me decade" is the parallel marriage. Such couples are often referred to as, "married singles." In a parallel marriage the husband and wife are going in many different directions, spending little quality time together. Gradually, they become strangers without even noticing the change. What seems like a marriage suddenly falling apart is really the inevitable result of couples growing slowly apart. Unfortunately, in today's society, a parallel marriage looks quite "normal." In this case "normal" is not good. A recent survey of married couples found that on the average, couples spent only thirty-seven minutes a week together *alone in meaningful communication.* Let me ask you a question. How can a successful marriage be built on thirty-seven minutes a week? The answer is simple . . . it can't.

---

[4]*U.S. News and World Report*, June 16, 1980, p. 49

4. Automatic Success Syndrome

Sydney J. Harris of the Field Newspaper Syndicate states the problem well, "Almost no one is foolish enough to imagine that he automatically deserves success in any field of activity; yet almost everyone believes he automatically deserves success in marriage."[5]

One of the greatest problems I see in the family today is that few people really believe that they must work at having successful marriages. Many Christians believe that being born again assures that their marriage will be a success. We are now very aware that this is a myth. Christian marriages can get into trouble very quickly.

5. Church Blindness

Let me quote from Gerald Dahl in his excellent book, *Why Christian Marriages Break Up*. "The purpose of the church 'remains unchanged.' The problem is that the church has become silent. Its passiveness toward troubled Christian marriages reflects a definite neglect of the authority given to it by God to shepherd its marriages and families."[6]

We must develop a definite plan to help Christian marriages in our churches if we are to reverse the trend toward unhappy marriages and divorce.

---

[5]*Readers Digest*, November 1980, p. 127.

[6]Gerald Dahl, *Why Christian Marriages Break Up;* (Nashville, Tennessee, Thomas Nelson Inc., 1979) p. 126. (Out of print.)

What Do Marriages Need?

I believe that there are foundational needs and functional needs of Christian marriages today. Let us look at the foundational needs first.

Biblical Framework

A Biblical framework for love and marriage is essential to working out a successful Christian marriage relationship. Following is an outline I use in teaching and counseling to help couples and individuals learn to think Biblically about love and marriage. This outline will work very well as a teaching handout. Feel free to copy the "Biblical Framework for Love and Marriage" for use within your church. This sheet can be used in counseling, premarital counseling, as part of a class on marriage, on a marriage retreat, or as a sermon outline.

Developing a Biblical Framework for Love and Marriage

World's View	Biblical View
Marriage	**Marriage**
1. Marriage can be temporary	1. Marriage is permanent (two exceptions—Matthew 19:3-9; Romans 7:2-4; 12; 1 Corinthians 7:39, 40)
2. Marriage is a secular contract	2. Marriage is a sacred covenant (Genesis 2:22-24; Matthew 19:3-6)

3. Marriage focuses on individual growth	3. Marriage focuses on oneness—unity in Christ, (Genesis 2:22-24; Ephesians 5:22-33) and the other's needs (Philippians 2:1-12)
4. The purpose of marriage is individual (my) happiness	4. Marriage is to glorify God and experience God's love in an intimate relationship (Ephesians 5:22-33; 1 Corinthins 10:31)
5. Marriage does not include male/female roles	5. Marriage includes male/female roles (Ephesians 5:22-33; 1 Peter 1:8)
6. Marriage may include procreation	6. Marriage includes procreation (Genesis 1:28)
7. Fidelity in marriage is not an absolute	7. Fidelity in marriage is an absolute (Exodus 20:14)
Love	**Love**
8. Love is conditional	8. Love is unconditional (1 John 4:7-11)
9. Love is primarily a feeling	9. Love is commitment, action, a decision (1 Corinthians 13; 1 John 3:16-18)
10. Love is primarily what brings me happiness.	10. Love is giving (1 John 15:12, 13; Ephesians 5:1, 2)

Marriage Work Ethic

The second foundational need in marriages today is a marriage work ethic. Marriages don't fall apart, they grow apart. Either a marriage is getting stronger or it is getting weaker. What is missing in most marriages is the knowledge that it takes work and a specific plan to have an abundant marriage. If we want to have a successful marriage, then we are going to have to spend the time and energy required to achieve it.

Functional Needs

We have just looked at foundational needs—those needs that form the base or foundation for a successful marriage. Now we will look at specific needs that can be built upon this solid foundation. These are the nitty-gritty skills, attitudes, and actions that make a marriage work. These needs are the structural part of building a marriage, and can be called "the functional needs."

To give us a handle on what some of the functional needs are, I would like to review two studies on marriage. This will help us isolate work areas for a marriage and develop ideas for providing enrichment within the church.

In 1980, *Redbook* magazine published a report of what marriage counselors believed to be the ten most common problems in marriages. That list is reprinted on the following page.

Redbook Study[7]

Your Rating

1. Breakdown in communication _____

2. Loss of shared goals and interests _____

3. Sexual incompatibility _____

4. Infidelity _____

5. Excitement and fun gone _____

6. Money _____

7. Conflict about children _____

8. Alcohol and drug abuse _____

9. Women's equality issues _____

10. In-laws _____

On the right side of the *Redbook* study I have given you a place to rank the problems you see as most common in marriages in your church. You may also use this list as a way of assessing the needs of individual couples in your church. Make a copy of this list and have couples rank the ten areas as to the order of importance in their own marriage. This will be helpful in designing your marriage enrichment curriculum.

A second helpful way to become aware of functional needs is to look at what makes successful marriages work.

---

[7]Claire Safran, *Redbook* Magazine, "Troubles that Pull Couples Apart"; (Redbook Pub. Co., New York, Jan. 1979) p. 83, 138.

In her book, *Married People: Staying Together in the Age of Divorce*,[8] Francine Klagbrun gives eight categories of abilities and outlooks that couples in strong marriage share. These are:

level of strength
in my marriage

Low Medium High

1. Enjoyment of Each Other
   (Based on doing things together, communicating)
   1 2 3 4 5 6 7 8 9 10

2. An Ability to Change
   (Adjusting to changing needs and situations in the marriage and family)
   1 2 3 4 5 6 7 8 9 10

3. An Ability to Live with the Unchangeable
   (Being able to accept imperfection in one another)
   1 2 3 4 5 6 7 8 9 10

4. An Assumption of Permanence
   (Do not see divorce as a viable option)
   1 2 3 4 5 6 7 8 9 10

5. Trusting Each Other
   (Each trusts the other that their core self will not be ridiculed or violated)
   1 2 3 4 5 6 7 8 9 10

6. A Balance of Dependencies
   (Partners are mutually dependent)
   1 2 3 4 5 6 7 8 9 10

7. A Shared and Cherished History
   (Partners build a meaningful history together)
   1 2 3 4 5 6 7 8 9 10

8. The Ability to be Lucky
   (Choosing the right person; not an epidemic of life crises)
   1 2 3 4 5 6 7 8 9 10

------

[8]Francine Klagbrun, *Married People: Sharing Together in the Age of Divorce*, Bantam

This list of eight categories can also be helpful to you in designing training opportunities for married couples and assessing their needs. Once again, you could have couples rate the level of strength in their own marriage. There is a scriptural base for most of these characteristics or attributes (number eight is a notable exception).

Ways to Meet Functional Marriage Needs

1. Create a Climate of Openness

An unwritten rule in many churches is that if people have family and marriage problems, they are to keep silent, and other church members are not to question them. Newcomers quickly learn that their problems are not to be discussed openly and so they suffer silently. With no place to receive support, counsel, and prayer, the problems grow until the church is "shocked" by yet another divorce or separation.

This should not be! Jesus was not reticent when facing personal problems. How would the woman at the well have been helped if Jesus had remained silent about her immoral life? The early church dealt openly with all kinds of personal/family/marriage issues. The many "one another" Scriptures indicate that the early church had a climate of openness—one where people could talk

In many churches, newcomers quickly learn that problems are to be kept to themselves.

about deep problems and receive help. They were not expected to put on a Sunday smile and act as if all was well.

I suggest that you make a conscious effort to create an open climate in your church. Let people know that they can have problems and still be loved and accepted. Let them know that they do not have to carry their marital burdens alone. It is a well-known fact that those who acknowledge marital and family problems and seek help have stronger marriages and families then those who do not. In the church, an integral part of building strong marriages and families is creating a climate of openness.

2. Make Premarital Counseling a Marriage Prerequisite

Develop a policy that makes premarital counseling a prerequisite to getting married in your church building. This preventive step is essential in any quality family ministry. In chapter four, I will give a comprehensive plan for premarital counseling.

3. Provide Marital Counseling

Every church should offer marriage counseling. However, many ministers are not equipped nor do they have the time for in-depth counseling. Many churches are finding that the answer to this dilemma is to refer people to Christian counselors in the area. Some have the counselor come to the church building for a certain number of hours each week. An arrangement is often made for a reduced fee, the counselor may give a discount, and/or the church may subsidize part of the cost with a special counseling fund.

4. Provide Marital Enrichment

The most important part of your ministry will be to prevent marital problems from developing. An ongoing program of marital enrichment is necessary to strengthen existing marriages and to build a strong framework for future marriages. I do not mean that marriage counseling (enrichment) will prevent all problems from occurring or solve all marriage problems. We have had couples go through three or four marriage-enrichment events, have marital counseling, and still get a divorce. As long as there are imperfect people, there will be imperfect marriages. Some will make wrong decisions. Our responsibility is to *offer* the opportunities to grow. We cannot take responsibility for those who decide to ignore the growth opportunities offered to them. Following are some ideas and resources for marriage enrichment.

Marriage Retreats and Classes—Marriage retreats and classes are basic ways of offering marital enrichment. Several books by H. Norman Wright have leader's guides and fit well into a class situation. These are: *Communication, Key to Your Marriage, The Pillars of Marriage,* and *More Communication Keys to Your Marriage* all produced by Gospel Light Publications.

At First Christian Church in Napa, California, we have developed a four-year ministry of marriage curriculum. The volumes we provide for each year are: *Understanding One Another, Loving One Another, Knowing One Another,* and *Delighting in One Another.* These manuals can be used in a class situation or on a marriage retreat. There are four to five chapters in each manual with group discussion questions at the end of each chapter. Couples read the chapter and answer the questions. The class or retreat consists of small groups of three to five couples with a group-leader couple. The groups discuss the questions for an hour and the couples then go off by themselves to complete a project based on the chapter and discussion. Complete information on how to order the manuals is in chapter eight.

Movies—There are two movie series on marriage that I think are excellent. One is Brecheen and Faulkner's *Marriage Enrichment* film series produced by Sweet Publishing Company. There is an accompanying study guide for personal and group use. Another is *Maximum Marriage,* a series of four films by Tim Timmons that our people thoroughly enjoyed. This film series produced by Merit Media International (contact your local Christian film distributor) also has an accompanying study guide. Movies are a good way to expose many people to marriage enrichment in a non-threatening way.

Couple's Night Out—Couple's night out is an idea for one evening of fellowship and marriage enrichment. Arrange for a place to get together—someone's home for dessert, or a restaurant—and then spend some time discussing a marriage topic. For example, someone could give an overview of a book such as Norm Wright's *Seasons of a Marriage* and the group could then discuss the principles.

Sermons on Marriage—A good way to demonstrate that the church puts a priority on enriching marriages is to have a series of sermons on marriage.

Seminars or Workshops on Marriage Enrichment Topics—The *Redbook* study and Francine Klagbrun's list of strong-marriage characteristics contained in this chapter will give you ideas for seminar or worship topics. For example, you could offer workshops on financial management (Larry Burkett wrote *Your Finances in Changing Times* and *How to Manage Your Money* published by Moody Press) or how to have husband and wife together times (*We Never Have Time for Just Us* published by Regal Books and written by Wayne Rickerson.)

Two excellent skill-building resources that fit into the seminar, workshop, or retreat format are *Couple Communication 1—Talking Together* from Interpersonal Communication Programs, Inc.

and *Training in Marriage Enrichment* from American Guidance Service. These are both secular resources that are compatible with Biblical principles. These resources are complete with couple's books and leader's guides. Full information on how to order them is in chapter four.

Books, Videos, Tapes—Make available books, videos and tapes on marriage enrichment topics (see resources in chapters seven and eight).

Outside Speakers—Invite speakers to share in their area of expertise. Compile a list of resource people in your area.

Reprints of Articles—There are excellent articles that appear in both Christian and secular magazines on marriage. Often you can get reprints of these or receive permission to reprint them yourselves. Make these reprints available to couples in your church.

Testimonies—Have testimonies in your church services from people with long-lasting, successful marriages and people who have faced and overcome specific difficulties in marriage.

Prayer Ministries—Challenge groups or individuals to have a ministry of prayer for couples in your congregation.

DISCUSSION QUESTIONS

1. Which of the five issues threatening marriages is most apparent among couples in your church?

2. Which world views of marriage and love do you observe among couples in your church? Which one do you believe is most destructive?

3. What do you think about the author's statement that to have a successful marriage, an old-fashioned work ethic is necessary?

4. Complete your rating on the *Redbook* study. In your opinion, what are the two most common problems in marriages?

5. Which of the eight categories of attitudes and abilities shared by couples in strong marriages is a strength in your marriage? In which area are you weakest?

6. How do you feel about your church creating a climate of openness? On a scale of 1-10, how open is your church body right now?

7. Does your church have a policy that requires premarital counseling?

8. Does your church have an affective marital counseling ministry?

9. Which marriage enrichment idea do you believe would best work for your church family?

PREPARING COUPLES FOR MARRIAGE

The belief that they will have a "happily ever-after" marriage is as strong in American teenagers today as it ever has been. A nationwide survey of 3,118 teens showed that ninety percent of the girls and eighty-five percent of the boys expect their marriage to last for life. But among 359 teens married or living with someone, only forty percent said their partnerships would last forever.[9]

Idealism causes blindness in several critical areas.

In this survey, we see the core of the happily ever-after syndrome—idealism. The term "love is blind" is not just a cliché when applied to premarital couples. Their idealism causes blindness in several areas that are critical in preparing couples for marriage. These are:

1) Premarital couples believe that getting married will resolve the problems they have in courtship. Studies indicate the opposite. Problems that couples have during engagement will be carried over into marriage. In addition, new problems will emerge.

2) Premarital couples have unrealistic expectations for themselves and one another. Most of these expectations are not discussed during engagement; they emerge after marriage often causing hurt and anger.

---

[9]*USA TODAY* newspaper, Nanci Hellmich, "Teens: Marriage Will Last Lifetime," March 25, 1985.

3) Premarital couples believe that their strong romantic feelings and high marital satisfaction will not diminish with time. The following graph shows the fallacy of this thinking.

Level of Marital Satisfaction*

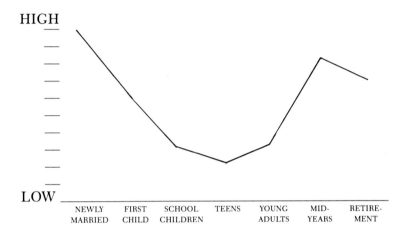

HIGH

LOW

| NEWLY MARRIED | FIRST CHILD | SCHOOL CHILDREN | TEENS | YOUNG ADULTS | MID-YEARS | RETIRE-MENT |

4) Many premarital couples believe that good marriages just happen naturally. This belief, unfortunately, is shared by many married couples. The truth of the matter is that a good marriage is achieved by placing a priority on the relationship.

Marriage—Still Popular

Marriage, as an institution, has survived the doomsday predictions of its demise. As imperfect as marriages are today, the vast majority of people are

---

*From *Family Careers—Developmental Change in Families* by Jane Aldous still opting for marriage. A 1978 *Newsweek* survey revealed that ninety-six percent will marry and of those, thirty-eight percent will divorce (that is higher now). Of those divorced, seventy-nine percent will remarry. Of those, forty-four percent will divorce again.[10]

Ninety-six percent of all couples are married in a religious ceremony, ninety-four percent have formal weddings. One third (843,000) of all weddings this year will be remarriages.[11]

As you can see, we are in a booming business! The potential for ministry is great. The *need* for ministry is even greater. In the church of our Jesus Christ, we have the resources available to help couples build strong Christian marriages.

The Churches' Responsibility

> *It is our responsibility to help couples build strong marriages.*

I believe it is the churches' responsibility to offer premarital counseling that will help couples build strong Christian marriages. "Most work with premarital couples today still continues to be done by clergy, who often feel inadequately trained and have insufficient time to work effectively with these couples before the marriage ceremony."[12]

---

[10]*Newsweek*, May 15, 1978

[11]*USA TODAY*, Richard David Story, Newlyweds: New Trends, Survey by Sunbeam Appliance Co., May 13, 1985.

[12]David Mace, *"How Effective is Marriage Preparation?"* (Prevention in Family Services, Sage Publishing, 1983) p. 65

The purpose of this chapter is to offer help for clergy and laity alike to work together to accomplish the enormous task of offering effective premarital enrichment in our churches.

What Are the Goals of Premarital Enrichment Counseling?

Premarital counseling should accomplish the following:

1) Build a close, on-going relationship between the couple and the person or persons doing the counseling.
2) Teach communication and conflict resolution skills.
3) Assess personality styles and how they fit together.
4) Help couples explore their expectations for one another and their marriage.
5) Provide a Biblical foundation for marriage.
6) Motivate the couples to place a high priority on building a strong Christian marriage.
7) Assist couples in developing a plan for spiritual growth—individually and together.
8) Provide information in such areas as sex, finances, family-of-origin issues, and in-laws.
9) Help the couples make a final decision on whether or not to marry.
10) Work out the details of the marriage ceremony.

While couples usually think they have made a final decision, research indicates that between thirty-five and forty-five percent of all engagements are terminated.[13] The premarital counseling procedure sometimes causes couples to re-evaluate their decision or postpone the wedding. On some occasions the person doing the premarital counseling cannot in good conscience marry the couple.

What Makes Premarital Counseling Effective?

More research need to be done on what makes the most effective premarital counseling, but the following research is helpful.

Number of Sessions

H. Norman Wright, in a study of 8,000 people who received premarital counseling from their church or pastor, discovered the following: Of those who had only one session, only fifteen percent said that it definitely helped their marriage. Thirty-two percent of those who had two sessions said that it definitely helped their marriage, while seventy-five percent of those who had seven or more sessions saw their marriages as having been definitely helped.

What we see from this survey is that for premarital counseling to effective, there must be more than two or three sessions. I highly recommend a minimum of eight sessions.

---

[13]H. Norman Wright, *Premarital Counseling;* (Chicago; Moody Press, 1977) p. 38.

Kind of Sessions

David H. Olson in the booklet, "How Effective is Marriage Preparation?" cited research that said, "It is clear that large lecture courses for groups of couples are not effective in helping premarital couples, no matter how well the lectures are presented."

Olson goes on to say that according to his research, effective premarital counseling includes the following three things:

1) A premarital inventory with a feedback session, or sessions.
2) Communication and conflict resolution skills.
3) Small support group where couples can share feelings and concerns with one another.

I would like to add to Dr. Olson's three components of effective premarital enrichment two more of my own:

4) Personality Assessment
5) Informational session (on such topics as included in goal eight on page forty-three.

Material Covered in Sessions

For premarital counseling to be effective, the material covered should be of a real and practical value to the couple. The eight sessions outlined below reflect what I have found to be useful. I am not suggesting that this is the final word on premarital counseling or that you should follow this exact pattern. Many of you (or your pastors) already have developed areas of premarital counseling that work well. Use the sessions I outline as a guideline and add what you believe will work well for you. There are others of you who will not be able to offer eight sessions to couples right now. Don't let that discourage you. Use what seems to you to be the most important sessions and add new ones as you are able. I suggest having one of the following sessions every two weeks.

Session One—Introduction/Getting Acquainted
Session Two—Personality Assessment
Session Three—Communication Skill Building
Sessions Four and Five—Prepare Inventory Feedback
Session Six—Family of Origin
Session Seven—Spiritual Life—Individually and Together, Goals for Marriage
Session Eight—Finances, Sex, etc.

Session One
Introduction and Getting Acquainted

The purpose of this first session is to get acquainted with the couple and lay the groundwork for the counseling. First, introduce yourself and share a little about your marriage and family. Next, ask them about their family backgrounds: How long have they lived at the present location, do they live alone or with parents, how many brothers and sisters do they have, do their parents approve of the marriage, and what is the marital status of their parents? If either has never lived alone (away from home), I suggest that you recommend that they move away from home even if for a few months. It is much more difficult to adjust to marriage when one or both individuals have never lived away from home.

Next, go over your marriage policy if you have one. If you do not have a written marriage policy, go over what you expect of them during these sessions. Explain the topics you will be covering. Ask what they would like to receive from the sessions.

Ask some questions about their dating background. How long have they known each other? How long have they been dating? How long have they been engaged? Ask why they believe this is the right time to get married and why they want to be married in the church. Ask, "Why do you want to marry this person?"

Give them the following materials, explain their purposes, and tell how each sheet is to be filled out. (I will explain how these are to be used as I go over each session.)

Personality Plus by Florence Littauer. This book deals with personality types—choleric, melancholy, phlegmatic, and sanguine—how to determine your own type, and how the types blend. The couple is to take the personality test on pages seventeen, eighteen, and nineteen, determine their temperament, and read the book for session two.

Couple Communication 1—Talking Together by Miller, Nunnally, and Wackman published by Interpersonal Communication Programs, Inc. (7201 South Broadway, Suite 6 Littleton, CO 80122). This book is to be read in advance for session three.

Prepare Inventory—To be returned at session two.

Family History Analysis—To be handed in at session five.

Becoming an In-law—Building Positive Relationships (Premarital couples give these sheets to their parents to fill out.) These should be returned by session six.

Session Two
Personality Assessment

In preparation for session two, the couple has taken the personality test in Florence Littauer's book. They should also have read the book. The purpose of this session is to review their personality styles and see how they fit together. The sheet on page fifty-four is for you to use during this session. This sheet will help the couple assess their differences, strengths, and weaknesses, and decide how they can blend them in marriage.

Another personality assessment tool that I have found useful in premarital counseling is the Taylor-Johnson Temperament Analysis. You are required to take a training session to qualify to use

this instrument. Christian Marriage Enrichment holds training sessions
throughout the United States. For more
information contact, Christian Marriage Enrichment, 1913 E. 17th Street,
Suite 118, Santa Ana, California,
92701.

Assignment for next session: Have the
couple read *Couple Communication
1—Talking Together* to prepare for the
next session. They are to memorize the
Awareness Wheel and be able to explain
how it works.

Session Three
Communication

The purpose of this session is to teach
the premarital couples some basics of
communication. The book they are to
read has a great tool to help them communicate. It is called the Awareness
Wheel. During this session have the
couple communicate with one another
over some issues using the Awareness
Wheel. Encourage the couple to use this
method of communication during the
following sessions.

Sessions Four and Five
Prepare Inventory Feedback

Prepare is an inventory for premarital
couples that provides a comprehensive
and clear picture of their strengths and
weaknesses in eleven critical areas of
marriage. These are:

1) Realistic Expectations
2) Personality Issues
3) Communication
4) Conflict Resolution
5) Financial Management
6) Leisure Activities
7) Sexual Relationship
8) Children and Marriage
9) Family and Friends
10) Equalitarian Roles
11) Religious Orientation

The Prepare Inventory is one of the most respected premarital tools available today. Norm Wright says, "I have found Prepare/Enrich to be the most helpful and informative tool ever published for helping couples as they prepare for their marriage."

A premarital couple takes the prepare inventory which consists of 125 items. You mail the completed forms to *Prepare/Enrich* and receive back a sixteen-page computerized printout that gives you a precise evaluation of the couple's weaknesses and strengths in the eleven areas. The printout is then your tool to use in helping the couples focus on their weak area. This will take from one to two sessions (usually two).

You can qualify to use *Prepare/Enrich* in two ways. There are training sessions held periodically throughout the United States and Canada. There is also a self-study method of qualifying if group sessions are not available in your area. For further information, write *Prepare/Enrich* P. O. Box 190, Minneapolis, MN, 55440, (612) 633-1027.

Assignment for session six: By now you should have received back from the couple their completed Family History Analysis forms and the Becoming an In-law forms from parents.

Session Six
Family of Origin

The families in which premarital couples were raised have a significant impact on their new marriage relationships. How affection was or was not shown in their home, how conflict was resolved, how they related to mother, father, brother, and sister, are just some of the areas that need to be explored. An effective tool to assist you in helping couples deal with their family of origin is the *Family History Analysis* developed by Norm Wright. Couples fill out this eight-page booklet and hand it back to you previous to session six. You then go over the booklet, marking areas that you believe are important for them to look at before marriage. During session six you will discuss the important areas you have discovered.

This simple, effective tool can be ordered from Christian Marriage Enrichment, 1913 E. 17th Street, Suite 118, Santa Ana, California, 92701, 714-542-3506. A leader's guide on how to use the *Family History Analysis* is included.

By session six you should have the "Becoming an In-law—Building Positive Relationships" sheets from the couple's parents. Give these forms to the couple for them to go over together after the session.

Assignment: To prepare for session seven, have the couple read Section 1, Step 6, "A Commitment to Plan for Shared Goals and Interests, Excitement in our Marriage, and Section 2, Fifty-two Husband/Wife Together Times, from the book, *We Never Have Time for Just Us* by Wayne Rickerson, Regal Books.

Session Seven
Spiritual Life, Individually and Together, Goals for Marriage

In session seven you will have an opportunity to share insights with the couples on how each can develop their own spiritual life and how they can develop their spiritual life together as a couple. This is also a good opportunity to share insights into Biblical roles of husbands and wives (Ephesians 5:22-33 and other related Scriptures).

The couples will have read about goal-setting and husband/wife together times in *We Never Have Time for Just Us*. Ask the couple what they plan to do to develop their spiritual life together.

Assignment for session eight: Give the couple the *Newly Married Budget Sheet*,* pages fifty-five and fifty-six. They are to fill this out and bring it to session eight.

Session Eight
Finances and Sex
(And whatever else you may need to discuss.)

The couple will have filled out their first-year budget sheet together. Some couples will be in such transition that this will be difficult for them to do. Encourage them, however, to fill in everything they possibly can. Go over the budget sheet with them and answer any questions or give any advice that you believe will be helpful.

Give the couples the tapes, "Before the Wedding Night" by Ed Wheat. These can be ordered from your local Bible book store. The couple is to listen to these tapes together. Additional resources for physical intimacy include *The Act of Marriage* by Tim LaHaye, Bantam Books; *Intended for Pleasure* by Ed Wheat, Revell; and *The Gift of Sex* by Cliff and Joyce Penner, Word.

If you are performing the marriage ceremony, use the remaining time in this closing session to discuss details of the wedding ceremony.

BLENDING PERSONALITIES
IN MARRIAGE

My personality style—
choleric, melancholy, phlegmatic, or sanguine

   Strengths _____

_____

   Weaknesses _____

_____

   Contribution to Marriage _____

_____

My fiancee's personality style _____

   Strengths _____

_____

   Weaknesses _____

_____

   Contribution to Marriage _____

How we complement one another _____

_____

_____

Possible conflicts _____

_____

_____

What I will do to accept and respect my fiancee's
   personality: _____

_____

_____

What I will do to modify my behavior to meet my fiancee's
personality needs: _____

_____

_____

NEWLY MARRIED BUDGET PLAN SHEET*

FLEXIBLE EXPENSES

Clothing $_____

Furniture and Equipment, including
  repairs   _____

Medical and Dental Care   _____

Contributions to Charity   _____

Gifts, Entertainment, Recreation,
  Hobbies   _____

Day-to-Day Living Costs

  Food and Household Supplies   _____

  Laundry and Cleaning   _____

  Drug Store Sundries   _____

  Books, Papers, Magazines   _____

  Car Upkeep   _____

  Personal Allowances   _____

    TOTAL FLEXIBLE EXPENSES $_____

Add all flexible expenses and divide by twelve. This
is the amount you need set aside each month to take
care of flexible expenses.

FIXED EXPENSES

Paycheck deductions for Taxes $_____

                Social Security   _____

                      Other   _____

Housing—Rent   _____

    Mortgage Payments   _____

    Taxes, Special Assessments   _____

Utilities—Gas   _____

            Electric   _____

            Phone   _____

            Water   _____

Church Support—Sunday Collections   _____

                     Special Collections   _____

Union or Professional Association Dues   _____

Membership Fees in Organizations   _____

Insurance Premiums   _____

Vehicle Licenses   _____

Regular Payments—Loans   _____

                     Installment Purchases_____

                     Christmas Savings

                          Club   _____

                          Other   _____

Regular Savings   _____

Add   TOTAL FIXED EXPENSES $_____

Then divide by twelve. This is the amount you will need
to set aside each month to take care of fixed expenses.

(1) Figure out you total income for your first year of mar-
    riage. (Total Annual Income) $_____

(2) Add your yearly flexible expenses and fixed expenses.
    (Total Annual Expenses) $_____

    Deduct two from one to find out if you are in the black
    or red. $_____

*Adapted from *The Christian Faces*, by Norm Wright,
Christian Marriage Enrichment, Denver, 1975, p. 80

BECOMING AN IN-LAW—
BUILDING POSITIVE RELATIONSHIPS

Please complete this form in detail by yourself. This information will be shared with the couple, during the last premarital counseling session.

1. Describe your relationship with your parents and in-laws during the early years of your marriage?
Parents:_____

_____

In-laws:_____

_____

2. Would you like your married children to approach you in the same way you approached your parents and in-laws? Why or why not?_____

_____

3. What would you list as some major needs of your soon-to-be-married son or daughter? Could these needs be best met 1) with your help, 2) by him or herself, or 3) with the new marriage partner?_____

_____

4. Are there some unique needs of your mate related to your child leaving? How might you help him or her in these areas?_____

_____

5. What will be your greatest adjustment that you will have to make as your son or daughter leaves home?

_____

6. If you could ask your son or daughter to pray for you as you make this transition, what would you ask them to pray?

_____

7. Will you expect them to visit you often? How do you define "often"? How will you go about suggesting that they visit you?_____

_____

8. When the newlyweds choose something that is not your choice, what do you think your response will be? (Can you think of an example?)_____

_____

9. Do you expect the newly married couple to call before visiting you and vice versa? Can there be spontaneous "drop-ins"?_____

_____

10. What plans, secrets, and problems do you expect the new couple to share with you? If this does not happen, what do you think your reaction will be?

_____

_____

11. In what way do you think and speak of your future son or daughter-in-law as a positive addition to your family?__

_____

12. In what way are you taking into consideration the feelings of the other family (parents-in-law) in:
making wedding plans_____

_____

scheduling holiday visits_____

_____

giving gifts_____

_____

seeing the grandchildren_____

_____

13. Please describe six expectations that you have for the couple after they are married._____

_____

14. Please take another piece of paper and together compose a letter describing, in detail, why you are looking forward to your son or daughter's fiancé becoming your son-or daughter-in-law. This should be addressed to this person. Please write at least three paragraphs.

Please return this form to the counselor or minister conducting the premarital preparation.

DISCUSSION QUESTIONS

1. What premarital preparation did you have for marriage? Did it help? What could you have used? What "blind" areas do you see in engaged couples in your church?

2. What does your church offer to premarital couples? Do you have a marriage policy?

3. What do you think about the author's statement that it is the church's responsibility to offer premarital counseling that will help couples build strong marriages?

4. Make a check mark by the goals of premarital counseling that your church is helping premarital couples work toward.

5. Outline what you would like to accomplish in premarital counseling.

6. List what you think should be included in a premarital policy for your church.

5

TEACHING PARENTS TO TEACH

Why Parents Need Training

"Children are a gift of the Lord; The fruit of the womb is a reward" (Psalm 127:3). Children also take an enormous amount of work and bring stress into the home. Surveys show that a couple's thoughts of divorce double after the first child.[16]

Parents need help in dealing with the many different challenges of rearing children in today's world. Many parents today do not have the extended families that once gave support and security to raising children. A young parent used to be able to talk to a mother, father, aunt, uncle, or other family member for support or advice. But families are more mobile today. Many couples no longer live close to relatives, or have long-established relationships in a community. There is simply no one to turn to when the children misbehave or the parents have questions about other issues.

"Children are a gift of the Lord," but also bring an enormous amount of work and stress into the home.

I was reminded of the stress that isolation causes when a young mother phoned me from an Indian reservation in Arizona. Her husband was employed by the government as a dentist on the reservation. The problem with their three-year-old girl was causing them tremendous stress. The answer to the problem was relatively simple, but this couple had no experienced parents to turn to. I'm sure that they could have found the answer they needed from friends or family if such a support group had been available.

Your church can provide the training and support to help such couples face the rigors of today's parenting.

I not only believe the church *can* provide such help, I believe we *must* provide such help. As local families of God, we have a great opportunity to become the extended families of those who desire such support. Scriptures tell us to "... encourage one another, and build up one another, just as you also are doing" (1 Thessalonians 5:11). God's Word also instructs us to "... consider how to stimulate one another to love and good deeds," (Hebrews 10:24). Parent-training and support groups can be valuable tools to encourage parents and stimulate them to good parenting in their homes.

Here at First Christian, we have offered parent training and support for the past six years. Not only has this been one of our best-attended family ministry activities, but also one of our most helpful. Participants have been very enthusiastic about the skills they have learned and the support they have received.

God's Word provides us with the foundation for effective parenting.

Three Vital Areas of Parent Training in the Church

Teach Biblical Precepts
God's Word provides us with the foundation for effective parenting. The

parenting precepts in Scripture keep us from getting caught up in the humanistic parenting propaganda being spread by family "specialists." Any resource or concepts we use from the human sciences must support—not contradict—God's Word. Human concepts about parenting come and go. God's precepts are eternal.

**Offering Training
in Seven Important Skills**

In addition to knowing and living out Biblical precepts of parenting, parents need training in specific parenting skills. This training should involve "hands on" methods, and information that will enhance parenting. I believe there are eight important skills for parents to learn. These are:

1. Developing a Positive Relationship With Children—learning the building blocks (time, focus, and acceptance) that produce close, loving relationships.
2. Understanding Development Stages in Children—knowing what to expect from a child at certain ages in terms of emotions, behavior, mental, and physical abilities.
3. Using Effective Methods of Discipline—being able to choose appropriate methods of discipline to fit the misbehavior.
4. Communicating Effectively—learning to use clear listening and speaking skills.

5. Enhancing Self-Esteem—learning how to relate to a child in such a way that his/her self-esteem is enhanced.
6. Building Family Togetherness—learning how to spend time together in a manner that forms close family ties.
7. Teaching Christian Values—teaching Godly values to the children. Helping them develop a life-style based on God's Word.
8. Learning to Adapt to Life-Cycle Changes—learning to deal with the stresses of having a first child, when the child goes to school, teenage years, and when the children leave home.

Provide Support for Parents

As we have already discussed, there is a great need for parent-support groups. While learning Biblical precepts and parenting skills is necessary, it is also important for parents to support one another. One of the most important things that happens in support groups is that parents learn that they are not bad parents, and that they do not have incorrigible children. This is often a great relief to parents.

Parents' needs for support vary. Single parents, stepparents, two original parents, parents of teens, and parents in pain (where children are delinquent or parents are facing a traumatic problem such as alcoholism, mental illness, or abuse) all have specific support needs that are unique to their situation.

There are many different ways to train parents in the church. Here are some that I have found to be effective:

1. Small Group Study and Support

An excellent way to provide both training and support is the Small Group Study and Support method. The group consists of six to ten parents with one person or couple as group leader(s). The group studies a chapter from a parenting book or manual and then meets to discuss what they have learned.

Here at First Christian we have developed four parenting manuals designed primarily for this method. These manuals are titled: *Help, I'm the Parent of a Preschooler, Help, I'm the Parent of a School-Aged Child, Help, I'm the Parent of a Teenager,* and *The Quibbling Sibling Survival Manual.* Each manual has six chapters with discussion questions at the end of each chapter. To prepare for the group, parents read the chapter and write out their answers to the discussion questions. The group session consists of parents sharing and discussing the answers to the questions. (These manuals are available for your use. For information on how to order them, write, Institute in Family Ministries, First Christian Church, 2659 First Street, Napa, CA 94558.)

The Small Group Study and Support method has several advantages. First, the lead person or couple doesn't have to

Small group support works well with parents who have special problems.

be an "expert." They are not on the spot because they prepare like the others in the group. Second, the parent receives initial input by reading the chapter. The "expert" then is the manual. Third, as each person answers the discussion questions, he/she receives an awareness of themselves. Fourth, when a person shares his or her answers with the group, he/she receives more personal awareness and input from others. Fifth, parents realize that they are not alone in their hurts and frustrations. Sixth, they feel the support and encouragement from others in the group. Seventh, they are encouraged to apply the principles to their family life.

We have found that it works well to hold these parenting groups once a week for six weeks. The actual group times should be an hour to an hour-and-a-half.

This format will work well with many books on parenting, with or without study guides. Pick out a book that you believe will meet the needs of parents in your church and write your own discussion questions for each chapter if no study guide is available. Then follow the procedures for group study as outlined here.

2. Small Support Group

Sometimes there is a need for parents to get together just for sharing and support. In this kind of group, there is generally no study assignments or discussion questions. This method involves more of, "This is what I'm going through," and "Here's what is helping me," kind of dialogue. The Small Support Group works well with parents who have special pressures, such as single parents, parents who have rebellious or delinquent teenagers, and couples who are blending families together.

3. Lecture and Involvement

Another excellent method is the Lecture and Involvement approach. This involves a resource person who gives instruction and then invites some kind of involvement such as projects, discussion application, or small group work. Lecture and Involvement works well in a class or seminar setting. David C. Cook Publishing Company has produced four parenting courses that use the Lecture and Involvement method. These are *Now We Are Three*, a course for parents-to-be and new parents by Eldon Fry, George Rekers and Judson Swihart; *Big people, Little People*, a course for parents of young children by Tom Eisenman; *You and Your Teen*, a course for mid-life parents by Charles Bradshaw, and *Just Me and the Kids*, a course for single parents by Patricia Brandt with David Jackson. These courses have teacher's guides, eighteen reproducible resource sheets for participants, and ten transparencies for overhead projection.

Another lecture and participation course that I highly recommend has been developed by the Baptist Sunday School Board. It is called, *Parenting by Grace, Discipline and Spiritual*

Growth. The leader's notebook includes an administrative guide, lesson plans, and worksheets for the participants. The parents (participants) also receive a workbook for personal study and projects to do at home with their children. This material, enough for an introductory lesson and ten more one-hour sessions, has been field-tested by 2,200 parents in twenty-seven states. The result is a quality product. For a free brochure, write, The Family Ministry Department, 127 9th Avenue North, Nashville, Tennessee, 37234, or call 615-251-2277.

Other Lecture and Involvement courses include: *How to Discipline and Build Self-Esteem in Your Child* by Betty Chase, a thirteen-session course published by David C. cook; *Building Positive Parent-Teen Relationships* by Norman Wright and Rex Johnson; *Preparing Youth for Dating, Courtship, and Marriage* by Norman Wright and Marvin Inmon; and *Help, We're Having a Baby (formerly called Preparing for Parenthood)*, by Norman Wright and Marvin Inmon (all three are available from Christian Marriage Enrichment, 714-542-3506).

4. Resources for Parents to Study

During the year I recommend many books and tapes for people to review on their own. People who are motivated to make changes or learn more about parenting benefit from these recommendations. Start a list of parenting resources you can recommend. Here are some parenting resources I have found to be particularly helpful:

HERE'S LIFE PUBLISHERS

When Love Becomes Anger by Kathy Collard Miller, (Controlling anger with children—good for the abusive parent as well as all parents who sometimes feel out of control.)

SCRIPTURE PRESS

Parents and Teenagers by Jay Kessler, Victor Books

STANDARD PUBLISHING

Check Your Homelife and *Bible Keys for Today's Family* by Knofel Staton, both available with leader's guides; *Listen to Your Children* by Marie Frost, leader's guide available; *Adventures in Being a Parent* by Shirley Pollock

TYNDALE

The Strong Willed Child by James Dobson

ZONDERVAN

Help, I'm a Parent by Bruce Narramore

The Readymade Family: How to be a Stepparent and Survive by Andre Bustanoby

The Hurting Parent by Margie M. Lewis

5. Videos and Films

Showing parents quality videos and films is another effective way to do parent training, however there are two obstacles to this approach. First, there are very few quality parent training films or videos available. Second, just showing film or video is not enough. There should be group work and application during or at the end of the film or video.

I have tried to review as many films and videos as possible and have found only one parenting course that I would use in my church. The Christian videos on parenting I have reviewed have been poor-to-terrible in quality. While some of the secular material available is of excellent quality, I believe it is too humanistic for evangelical Christians to use.

The exception in Christian parenting videos is *Famous Fathers* produced by David C. Cook. I believe this is an outstanding, informative and inspirational course for training fathers. There are four videos in the series, a leader's guide, and participant workbooks. I highly recommend this series.

James Dobson's, *Focus on the Family* is a high-quality film series that includes parenting issues. Many churches have used this film series and it is now available in video cassette.

6. Personal Discipleship

In Titus, Paul urged older women to " . . . encourage the young women to love their husbands, to love their children" (Titus 2:4). This principle of discipleship, that an older or a more experienced person may help a younger person, is as valid today as it was in Paul's time. Parents going through

This principle of discipleship is as valid today as it was in Paul's time.

problems with their children can benefit from the personal discipleship of
someone who has already been down
that road. When parents in your church
need specific help, direct them toward
older parents who have learned valuable parenting lessons through experience.

7. Counseling

Some parenting problems are best
handled through family or personal
counseling. If the problems seem more
complex than your training allows you
to handle, then refer the people to a
professional counselor. Find someone in
your community who specializes in
child, adolescent, and/or family counseling.

Conclusion

Parent training in the church gives us
a wonderful opportunity to meet specific needs. You do not have to start with
a full-blown program. Begin small and
build. For example, the first year you
might want to offer one class, or purchase several books on vital parenting
topics for parents to check out and read.
As the program grows, you will find
that parent training can be one of your
most rewarding ministries.

DISCUSSION QUESTIONS

1. What challenges do parents face today that they did not face fifty years ago?

2. How do you see the lack of extended family support affecting families in your church?

3. In which of the three vital areas of parenting do parents in your church need the most help?

4. What opportunities for support does your church offer parents?

5. Which of the different methods for training parents do you believe would work best in your church?

6. What parent training could you do in your church this year?

6

ENABLING PARENTS TO TEACH

There was a time when the only place children learned religious values was in the home. Think back to the time of Abraham. There were no Bible schools, no youth groups, no Christian schools— not even any corporate worship. In the Old Testament times, the only way children learned about God and how to lead a Godly life-style was from their parents.

Psalm 78 reveals just how important

the family was in the transmission of religious values from generation to generation.

> "For He established a testimony in Jacob,
> And appointed a law in Israel,
> Which He commanded our fathers,
> That they should teach them to their children;
> That the generation to come might know,
>   even the children yet to be born,
> That they may arise and tell them to their children,
> That they should put their confidence in God,
> And not forget the works of God,
> But keep His commandments,
> And not be like their fathers,
> A stubborn and rebellious generation,
> A generation that did not prepare its heart,
> And whose spirit was not faithful to God."
>
> (Psalm 78:5-8)

Throughout the Old and New Testaments, the family remains the primary instrument for the teaching of Christian values. God in his infinite wisdom knew that the best place for children to learn of Him was in the loving atmosphere of a home.

God, in His infinite wisdom, knew that the home was the best place for children to learn of Him.

The Church Replaces the Family

During the last 200 years the church has slowly replaced the home as the place where Christian values are taught. With the development of the Sunday school and other subsequent Christian education programs, parents began to feel less and less responsible for teaching their children.

Anna B. Mow discusses this phenomenon in her book *Your Child*. "The late Dr. C.C. Ellis of Juniata College wondered one day why some of the devout Christian leaders of the last century should have objected to the Sunday-school movement. Why did they object to the church teaching religion to the children? Alert scholar that he was, he went to the archives of old Eastern Pennsylvania churches to find what reasons they gave in their council meeting minutes for such objections. To his astonishment it was not that they were reluctant to take on something new. Instead he found their recorded objection to be, "If the church takes up the teaching of the children, the homes will let it go and will leave the responsibility to the church."[16]

Why did devout Christian leaders object to Sunday school?

I am afraid that those old church leaders were correct. It seems to me that parents have abandoned the teaching of Christian values and expect the church to fill the void.

Partners Together in Education

The church and family working together can be a powerful team in teaching Christian values to children. The educational agencies of the church can be wonderful support systems for the home. Children can learn Christian values from adult models other than their

---

[16]Anna B. Mow, *Your Child*; (Grand Rapids, Zondervan Publishing House, 1963) p. 23

parents. They can learn in groups with peers. The church's educational agencies, however, should never take the place of parents. The parents remain primarily responsible for teaching Christian values to their children. The church should support and enrich what is already happening in the home.

This may all seem rather idealistic, but we must keep the Biblical model before us. I know that not all families are going to act on their Biblical responsibility, but some will. There are children who do not have Christian parents and we have a responsibility for their Christian education. The church's responsibility is to equip those parents who are willing to teach Christian values in the home. This equipping should include an emphasis on Biblical principles of teaching Christian values, and creative methods an resources to make this teaching effective.

Values, whether important to us or to God, are proven by our actions.

Enabling Parents to Teach Christian Values

Following is a plan to help you enable parents in your church to teach Christian values to their children. I suggest using the material in this chapter in a two-hour seminar for parents. This seminar on how to teach Christian values in the home involves three steps:

Step One—Your Values. This step will help parents understand what a Christian value is and evaluate their own values system.

Step Two—How to Teach Christian Values. Step two gives the Biblical principles for teaching Christian values in the home.

Step Three—Teaching Christian Values Through Family Times. Step three shows parents creative ways to teach Christian values through family times.

Preparing for the Seminar

In advance of offering this seminar or class to parents, you will need to do the following: Duplicate enough response sheets (found at the end of this chapter) for each person taking the training. You will notice that there are three response sheets, one for each step. Parents will fill in certain information as your proceed through the seminar.

Order some family activity materials for the parents to purchase. You might want to charge a fee for the seminar and give the materials as part of that fee. I have written a series of activity manuals that will work well for this purpose. These activity manuals are, *Preschoolers, Christian Family Activities for Families with School Age Children,* and *Christian Family Activities for Families with Teens.* Three more from Standard Publishing include: *Christian Family Activities for Single Parent Families* by Donna Read, *Fun Ideas for Family Devotions* by Ginger Jurries and Karen Mulder, and *Family Fun Times* by Wayne Rickerson.

Each of these manuals contains approximately a year's worth of family activity material (if the activities are used once a week) and Biblical principles on teaching Christian values within the home. In addition, I recommend *Together at Home*, by Dean and Grace Merrill, (from Thomas Nelson Publishers, and *Our Christmas Handbook* by Sharon Lee, also from Standard Publishing.

The Seminar:
How to Teach Christian Values in the Home

Step One
Identifying Your Values
(Sixty Minutes)

Goal—to help parents understand the meaning of Christian values and determine their own values by listing them. Give everyone the resource sheet "Step One—Your Values." As the participants fill out this sheet, give them the following information:

1. What Are Our Values?
(Five Minutes)
   A value is something you believe is very important. A Christian value is something God believes is important. Our real values are proven by our actions. For example, honesty is a true value only when we fill out our income tax forms honestly. Often we say we have values but our actions contradict our words.

God's greatest values are given in Matthew 22:36-40. (Read or have someone read these verses.) God's greatest values are 1) love of God, 2) love of neighbor and 3) love of self (inferred).

2. *Brain Bust on Values* (Ten Minutes)

Have the group list as many values as they can think of. Write these on a chalkboard or overhead transparency as they are given.

3. *List Ten Greatest Values* (Twenty Minutes)

Have participants list their ten greatest values in the appropriate space on the response sheet. This will be very difficult for some because they have never thought in such specific terms about what they hold important.

After they have listed their ten values, they should write a Scripture that gives a Biblical base of each value. The final step in this exercise is to rate themselves on how well they model that value. For example, if one of the values was self-discipline, a person might list 1 Timothy 4:7 for the Scripture and eight for a self-rating. That would mean they would be rating themselves as being very well disciplined.

4. *Small Group Activity* (Fifteen Minutes)

Form small groups of five or six people. Have the people in each group share with one another the two most important values they would like to teach their children. They should share why they chose those two and how well they themselves are doing in living out that value.

Give participants a ten-minute break.

Step Two
How to Teach Christian Values
(Forty Minutes)

Goal—To help parents see their responsibility to teach Christian values and have them learn the three principles of teaching Christian values in Deuteronomy 6:4-9.

Give each parent the resource sheet "Step Two—How to Teach Christian Values." Give the following information as they fill out their sheets:

1. *Biblical Principles for Teaching Christian Values* (Thirty Minutes)

Divide seminar participants into groups of six to eight and have them read Deuteronomy 6:4-9 and answer the following questions:

Who is to teach? How is the teaching done? (Instruct them to fill in the circle with three ways of teaching). Why does God want parents to teach? Where does the church fit in?

After the participants have discussed these questions for fifteen minutes, have a report from each group. After each group has expressed its opinions, give any of the following information they might have missed.

Who is to teach? It is obvious from the text that Moses is speaking directly to parents.

How is the teaching to be done? In Deuteronomy 6:4-9 there are three principle methods by which to teach Christian values. First parents are to *model*—teaching by example, second they are to *teach*—which is formal or structured teaching, and they are to *talk*—which is informal teaching.

Model (Deuteronomy 6:4, 5)

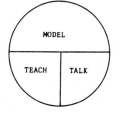

Verses four and five say that parents are to first love God and have the words which are being commanded this day in their own hearts. The most powerful teaching principle of all is given first in this passage. God's Word must be first in parent's lives if they are to effectively teach it to their children. Children learn from what they see us do. If they hear us say one thing and do another, our teaching will be ineffective.

Teach (Deuteronomy 6:7a)

Parents were to *teach* God commandments diligently to their children. In the word Hebrew, "teach" suggests a structured teaching situation, a time set aside by parents to explain God's Word to their children ... family nights, family activities that involve God's Word, and other kinds of family devotions are an example of this principle.

Talk (Deuteronomy 6:7b-9)

Parents were to also talk to their children about God's Word. This suggests an informal kind of teaching that occurs throughout the day, "sitting, lying down, walking, and getting up." In other words, look for the teachable moment and apply God's Word to everyday circumstances.

These three principles should compose a life-style for parents.

All three principles should be used when teaching children. These three principles should compose a teaching life-style for parents.

Why does God want parents to teach? There are many reasons. Parents care more about the child than anyone else. Parents have more opportunities— more time with the children. Parents grow in maturity when they teach their own children (the teacher always learns the most). Parents have the opportunity to model what they teach on a consistent basis. Whatever the reasons, parents are commanded by God to teach their children.

Where does the church fit in? The church should equip parents to teach Christian values to their children. The church also has a responsibility to children who do not have Christian parents. And, the church has a wonderful opportunity to provide other models for children. Youth groups and Bible-school classes offer children opportunities to learn additional Bible content and applications as they observe the lives of their teachers and the other adults in the church.

It is our responsibility to equip parents to teach Christian values to their children.

How do you rate? (Five Minutes) Have parents rate themselves on their response sheet in the areas of model, teach, and talk.

Step Three
Teaching Christian Values Through Family Times
(Thirty Minutes)

Goal—To help parents see the potential of teaching Christian resources to have successful family times in their own homes.

Give each parent the resource sheet "Step Three—Teaching Christian Values Through Family Times." As they fill in their sheets give the following information:

1. *Family Times are Effective*

Family times are an effective way to teach Christian values because: (Expand on each area below from your own experience or from your reading):

—Family times promote *togetherness.*
—Family times provide an opportunity to teach God's Word in creative ways.
—Family times are an excellent time to *apply* God's Word.
—Family times meet the *needs* of children.

2. *Keys to Successful Family Times*

Commitment   Parents must commit themselves to regular family times to make them successful. I suggest a once a week family night. Our family has had family nights for twelve years and we have found these an excellent way to have fun, promote family togetherness, and teach Christian values.

Above all, make having fun your highest priority.

Fun   By all means, make having fun your highest priority. If you don't make this a fun time you will probably stop having family times.

Participation Be sure to allow each family member to participate in your family times. Let one child serve or make dessert. Let another child lead a game or activity. Take turns reading the Bible or Bible storybook. Each family member should have something to do each family time. You might want to alternate having a different family member each week be in charge of the family time.

Flexibility and Variety Do lots of different things during your family times. The resources given will help you have fun while teaching Christian values. Besides the activities in these resources, do other kinds of things. Do outdoor activities during the summer, carve pumpkins together the week of Halloween, go to various events and places together. Make a list of fun things your family can do together.

Step Four
Role Play a Family Night

Hand out family activity manuals and divide your group into "families" of four or five. Have a father, mother, and two or three children. Choose a family activity out of the books for each "family" to do. Have them do the activity playing the various roles they have been assigned.

After the role play, have a feedback session on how they enjoyed the family activity. Allow for questions on any part of the material you have presented.

CHRISTIAN VALUES RESPONSE SHEET
STEP ONE—YOUR VALUES

1. (Five Minutes)
What is a value?

_____

_____

What is Christian value?

_____

_____

A real value is _____

_____

God's greatest values are given in Matthew 22:34-40. They are (1) love of _____ (2) love of _____ (3) love of _____

2. (Ten Minutes)
Brain Bust on Values

_____

_____

_____

_____

_____

_____

3. (Thirty Minutes)
List the ten values that you would most like your children to
have. List these in the order of importance. Next, list a
Biblical base for that value. Finally, rate how well you
model that value on a scale of one to ten with ten being
perfect.

Value	Scripture	How I Rate
1. _____	_____	1 2 3 4 5 6 7 8 9 10
2. _____	_____	1 2 3 4 5 6 7 8 9 10
3. _____	_____	1 2 3 4 5 6 7 8 9 10
4. _____	_____	1 2 3 4 5 6 7 8 9 10
5. _____	_____	1 2 3 4 5 6 7 8 9 10
6. _____	_____	1 2 3 4 5 6 7 8 9 10
7. _____	_____	1 2 3 4 5 6 7 8 9 10
8. _____	_____	1 2 3 4 5 6 7 8 9 10
9. _____	_____	1 2 3 4 5 6 7 8 9 10
10. _____	_____	1 2 3 4 5 6 7 8 9 10

4. (Fifteen Minutes) Small Group Activity

Share your top two values with others in the group.

CHRISTIAN VALUES RESPONSE SHEET
STEP TWO—HOW TO TEACH CHRISTIAN VALUES

1. (Twenty Minutes)
   Biblical Principles for Teaching Christian Values
   Group read Deuteronomy 6:4-9 and answer the following questions:

   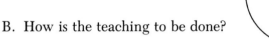

   A. Who is to teach?

   B. How is the teaching to be done?

   C. Why does God want parents to teach?

   D. Where does the church fit in?

2. (Fifteen Minutes)
   Three Principles of Teaching Christian Values

3. (Five Minutes)
   How do you rate in each area?

	low	med.	high
Model	1 2 3 4 5 6 7 8 9 10		
Teach	1 2 3 4 5 6 7 8 9 10		
Talk	1 2 3 4 5 6 7 8 9 10		

CHRISTIAN VALUES RESPONSE SHEET THREE
TEACHING CHRISTIAN VALUES
THROUGH FAMILY TIMES

1. —Family times are an effective way to teach
   Christian values because:
   —Family times promote family _____
   —Family times provide an opportunity to teach God's
     Word in _____ ways
   —Family times are an excellent time to _____
     God's Word
   —Family times _____ the needs of children

2. Keys to Successful Family Times:
   1. _____
   2. _____
   3. _____
   4. _____

3. Resources to Use for Family Times
   1. *Christian Family Activities for Families with Pre-
      schoolers*
   2. *Christian Family Activities for Families with School
      Age Children*
   3. *Christian Family Activities for Families With Teens*
   4. *Christian Family Activities for Single Parent Families*
      by Donna Read)
   5. *Fun Ideas for Family Devotions* by Ginger Jurries and
      Karen Mulder;
   6. *Family Fun Times* by Wayne Rickerson
   7. *Our Christmas Handbook* by Sharon Lee. (All of the
      above are from Standard Publishing.)
   8. *Together at Home* by Dean and Grace Merrill (From
      Thomas Nelson Publishers.)

4. Our Plan for Family Times
   What day or days _____
   What resources _____
   What values _____

5. Role Play a Family Night

DISCUSSION QUESTIONS

1. The author states that the church has replaced the family as the place where Christian values are taught. Do you agree or disagree with that statement?

2. How does your church help parents teach Christian values to their children? Is your family in partnership with the church in education?

3. The author gives a seminar outline to help equip parents to teach Christian values. Do you believe this seminar would be successful in your church?

7

DEVELOPING A RELATIONAL CURRICULUM

As this is written, the number-one, best-selling, non-fiction paperback in the nation is *The Road Less Traveled*, by Dr. Scott Peck. This is particularly unusual in a time when best-sellers generally concern celebrities or cellulite, because Peck's book not only calls for a higher life-style but also has religious overtones. It is most unusual for a number-one best-seller to start with such a negative opening as, "Life is difficult."

Peck, who started the book as an unbeliever and has since found faith in God, gives the following explanation for the phenomenal success of his book,

"People are thirsting for integrity. What's attracting them to my work is their desire to integrate religion into the rest of their lives."[17]

---

[17]*Newsweek*, November 18, 1985 p. 79

The New Road to Be Traveled

The new road to be traveled in churches is to help Christians integrate their faith into the rest of their lives. The road less traveled must become the road more traveled in our churches today if Christians are to live truly abundant lives. As I mentioned in chapter one, we now have a new function of the family. That function is relational. As never before, people need help in applying God's truth to their relationships. They want to know how to develop their relationships with their spouse and children, how to resolve conflict, how to overcome depression, how to manage anger, how to get along with difficult people, etc. As a church, we have the responsibility and opportunity to pave this new road with insights that can make the journey successful.

The Relational Foundation

A relational curriculum must have as its foundation a relational theology. In chapter one I discussed how the central doctrine of the Bible, love, deals with three basic relationships: a person's relationship with God, his relationship with others, and his relationship with himself (Matthew 22:37-39). Any relational curriculum that a church develops will always be helping people develop Biblical attitudes and functional skills in those three areas.

A Relational Curriculum

A dynamic way to help people on the road they must travel to an abundant relationship with God, self, and others, is to start developing a relational curriculum in your church. Actually, the entire theme of this book is about building a relational curriculum. Until now, however, we have been dealing with a relational curriculum that applied directly to various aspects of family life. Now we are expanding our horizons to include relational issues that affect people both inside and outside of marriage and family.

Where Do People Need Help?

People today have an enormous need for relationship skills. I would like to list some of the areas in which people need help in order to expand your vision as to the opportunities your church can have. In some cases I will suggest resources. Some of these resources are Christian and others are secular. When using the secular resources, I suggest integrating Scripture into the principles you are teaching. There is often a Biblical base for these principles.

Life Cycle Issues

There are certain cycles, or stages, that most of us will go through in our lifetime. We add new roles (becoming a new parent) or lose old roles (last child leaves home). Each change of roles is called a life cycle. Each new stage brings with it times of stress and instability. Every life cycle represents a relationship need. People need to know how to deal with themselves and others as the new roles develop and diminish. People need informational support during these critical stages. The relational curriculum of the church can help people work through these important times.

Dennis Guernsey, associate professor and director of Marriage and Family Ministries at Fuller Theological Seminary, has written extensively about how the church can minister to individuals during life cycle changes in his book, *A New Design for Family Ministry*. Dr. Guernsey, in cooperation with David C. Cook Publishing Company, has developed a life cycle curriculum that includes three stages. I have already recommended some of these courses but I will now list the entire curriculum. Each curriculum piece addresses a life cycle need.

1. The between-families young adult course: *On My Own, A Course for Young Singles* by Tom Eisenman.
2. Newly married young adults course: *Newly Married, A Course to Build Foundations* by Wayne Rickerson
3. The first child and preschool children course: *Now We Are Three, A Course for Parents-to-Be and New Parents* by Eldon Fry, George Rekers, and Judson Swihart.

> *The church can help people learn how to deal with themselves and others during stressful life cycles.*

4. Families with young children course: *Big People, Little People, A Course for Parents of Young Children* by Tom Eisenman.
5. The first teenager through launching course: *You and Your Teen, a Course for Mid-Life Parents* by Charles Bradshaw.
6. Launching and middle years course: *Empty Nest, Life After the Kids Leave Home* by Earl Wilson.
7. The retirement years course: *The Freedom years, A Celebration of Retirement* by Larry Ferguson with David Jackson.
8. The single person and single parent course (this is technically not a stage but is included in these courses because of the great need): *Just Me and the Kids, A Course for Single Parents* by Patricia Brandt with David Jackson.

Anger

Anger is something that all Christians deal with and yet it is seldom a topic in the church. How we manage our anger is a key to many of our relationships. I do not know of any courses, but the books *Overcoming Hurts and Anger* by Dwight L. Carlson (Harvest House Publishers) and *The Rights and Wrongs of Anger* by H. Norman Wright (Harvest House Publishers) are both excellent resources.

Depression

This has been called the age of depression. Christians need to know how to deal with depression in their lives. *Resources: Now I Know Why I'm Depressed* by H. Norman Wright (Harvest House Publishers): *Feeling Good: The New Mood Therapy* by David D. Burns, M.D. (Morrow, 1980—secular).

Crisis

Two excellent secular books that could be the basis of a small group discussion or class are *Living Through Personal Crisis* by Ann Kaiser Stearns (Ballantine 1985), and *How Can It Be All Right When Everything is All Wrong?* by Lewis B. Smedes (Harper & Row Publishers, 1982).

Men in Mid-Life Crisis by James Conway (David C. Cook Publishing Co., 1978 and *Women in Mid-Life Crisis* by James & Sally Conway (Tyndale House Publishers, 1983). Secular Resource: *The Forty to Sixty-Year-Old Male* by Michael E. McGill, Ph.D (Simon and Schuster, 1980).

Assertiveness

Beyond Assertiveness by John C. Faul and David Augsburger (Word, Inc. 1980) This book provides a Biblical base for assertiveness.

Personality Differences

People need to understand their personalities and how their personalities blend with others. I recommend *Personality Plus* by Florence Littauer (Power Books, Revell Co., 1982); *Irregular Peo-*

ple by Joyce Landorf (Word, Inc. 1982); and *Dealing With Difficult People* by Charles Keating (Paulist Press, 1984).

Sex
The Gift of Sex by Clifford and Joyce Penner (Word, Inc., 1981); *The Act of Marriage* by Tim and Beverly Lahaye (Zondervan Publishing house, 1979); *Solomon on Sex* by Joseph Dillow (Thomas Nelson, Inc., 1978); and *Love Life for Every Married Couple* by Ed Wheat (Zondervan, 1980).

Controlling Thoughts and Emotions
Self-Talk: Key to Personal growth by David Stoop (Fleming H. Revell, 1981) and *Refresh Your Marriage with Self Talk* by David and Jan Stoop (Fleming H. Revell, 1984). Secular Resource: *Feeling Good: the New Mood Therapy* by David D. Burns, M.D. (Morrow 1980); *No Condemnation: Rethinking Guilt Motivation* by Bruce Narramore (Zondervan, 1984)

Finances
Your Finances in Changing Times and *How to Manage Your Money* both by Larry Burkett (Moody Press, 1982)

Stress
Stress/Unstress by Keith W. Sehnert, M.D. (Augsburg, 1981); *Life Stress: Winning the Battle in 30 Days* by Don Osgood (Here's Life); *Living With Stress* by Lloyd H. Ahlem (Regal Books,

1982). Secular Resource: *The Relaxation and Stress Reduction Workbook* by Martha Davis and Matthew McKay (New Harbinger, 1982).

Type A Behavior

Many Christians have Type A behavior. This often limits joy in the Christian life. A secular book dealing with this subject is *Treating Type A Behavior: And Your Heart* by Meyer Friedman and Diane Ulmer, (Alfred A. Knopf, 1984).

Self-Disclosure

Fully Human, Fully alive, The Secret of Staying in Love, and *Why Am I Afraid to Tell You Who I Am?*, all by John Powell (Argus).

Tough Love

Love Must Be Tough by James Dobson (Word, Inc.); *Toughlove*, a secular book especially for parents of rebellious teens by Phyllis and David York and Ted Wachtel (Bantam, 1983).

Goals/Successful Living

Strategy for Living, by Edward Dayton and Ted Engstrom (Gospel Light/ Regal); *The Pursuit of Excellence* by Ted W. Engstrom (Zondervan, 1982): *The Sensation of Being Somebody* (self-esteem), by Maurice E. Wagner (Zondervan, 1979); *You're Someone Special* by Bruce Narramore (Zondervan, 1980).

Dealing With Emotions

Living With Your Emotions—Self Image and Depression, a curriculum by H. Norman Wright (Harvest House); *The Healing of Fears* by H. Norman Wright (Harvest House); *Healing for Damaged Emotions* by David Seamands (Victor Books/Scripture Press, 1981); *Putting Away Childish Things* by David Seamands (Victor Books/Scripture Press, 1982); and *Making Peace With Your Past*, by H. Norman Wright (Revell).

Forgiveness

Caring Enough to Forgive by David Augsburger (Regal Books/Gospel Light, 1981); *Caring Enough to Forgive/Caring Enough Not to Forgive* by David Augsburger (Herald 1981); *The Freedom of Forgiveness* by David Augsburger (Moody, 1970) and *Love, Acceptance and Forgiveness* by Stanley Baldwin and Jerry Cook (Regal, 1979).

Communication/Conflict Resolution

Caring Enough to Confront by David Augsburger (Herald, 1980) and *Couples Communication 1—Talking Together* by Sherod Miller, Elam W. Nunnanlly, and Daniel B. Wackman (Interpersonal Communications Program Inc., 1984)

In-Law Relations

How to Be a Better-Than-Average In-Law by H. Norman Wright (Victor Books/Scripture Press, 1981)

Death and Dying/Grief

The Last Thing We Talk About by Joseph Bayly (David C. Cook); *On Death and Dying* by Elisabeth Kubler-Ross (Macmillan, 1969) and a good section in *Training Christians to Counsel* by Norman Wright (Harvest House, 1983); *What You Should Know About Suicide* by Bill Blackburn (Word, 1982).

Physical Health

Fit or Fat? by Covert Bailey (Houghton Mifflin, 1977).

Divorce Recovery

Growing Through Divorce by Jim Smoke (Harvest House, 1982) and *Beyond Divorce* by Brenda Hunter (Revell, 1979).

DISCUSSION PROMPTER

Design a relational curriculum for your church. Select ten topics and resources you believe people in your church need to cover.

IDEAS FOR YOUR FAMILY MINISTRY

In this book I have tried to maintain a balance between Biblical foundations, family ministry theory, and hands-on tools for use in the local church. Until now I have given ministry ideas that fit with the topic of the chapters. In this chapter I am going to give you a wide range of ideas that will fit many types of situations.

However you choose to use these ideas, it is important to always keep your purpose clearly in mind. Your family ministry needs to move toward specific goals. When deciding which of these ideas to use, your family ministry committee needs to see if that idea helps you move toward your stated purposes and goals. Don't be tempted to use an idea just because it is exciting and you think your people will enjoy it.

The following ideas are to help you

Always keep your purpose in mind. Your family needs to move toward specific goals.

expand your vision of family ministries and stimulate your own creativity. Use the ideas that will enable you to reach your purposes and goals.

1. Food and Fellowship Forums

At First Christian we wanted a way to reach a wider range of people than we were helping through our seminars, retreats, and classes. To accomplish this, our Family Ministry Committee developed the concept of Food and Fellowship Forums. We decided that the Food and Fellowship Forum would be informal in nature, held in homes, and would focus on issues pertaining to the family or personal growth.

Our forums start at 6:30 on Saturday evenings and are held approximately once a month. People bring potluck dishes and we spend about an hour fellowshiping over food. At 7:30-7:45 we start our input time. At the forums, we generally feature a film, video, or special speaker. We have had speakers on such topics as developing self-esteem, communication, stages in a marriage, and personality styles in marriage. Sometimes we use outside speakers and other times our own staff or lay people speak.

The strength of Food and Fellowship Forums is that you can give valuable family relational input to people in a non-threatening environment of fellowship. Because of the simple format, these forums are relatively easy to plan and administer.

2. Ten Dates for Mates

Ten Dates for Mates is a book written by Dave and Claudia Arp (Thomas Nelson, publisher). The content of the book is just what the title says; ten dates for mates. The ten dates cover ten critical areas of marriage and give couples a plan for working on those areas in their marriage. The couple sets a date to read the material, discuss it, and apply it to their marriage relationship.

I suggest using the book in the following way: Advertise that you will be giving away a free book, *Ten Dates for Mates*. Mention that to receive this book, couples must promise to read it and have at least one date.

Schedule a "Ten Dates for Mates" evening. Spend time with the couples going over the value of setting aside specific times to work on marriage relationships. Give out the books and go over one of the dates with the couples so they can see how the plan works. Schedule another meeting in two months when the couples will come back and talk about the outcome of their first date.

3. Family Life Resource Center.

Start a Family Life Resource Center in your church. This will be a place where individuals and families can check out books, audio tapes, video tapes, games, etc., to help their family life and personal development. For some churches, this could be a special addition to their library or media center. The resources listed in this book will be helpful in starting your Family Life Resource Center. Use a part of your family ministries budget to add resources each year.

4. Family Vacation Bible School

I see family vacation Bible schools as a good way to help families. Family vacation Bible schools are usually held in the evening during the summer. There are various ways to organize these. One way is to keep families together during the entire evening. A family would do projects together and then interact with other families in a family cluster (three to five families).

A second way to have a family vacation Bible school is to separate family members into age groups part of the time, and have them meet together as families part of the time. For example, the first hour the children and youth could study with their own peer groups and the adults could study family-related electives. The last hour would be spent with families working together on family-related projects. I have found it effective to have individual families do projects together (the *Christian Family Activity* books work well) and then share the results of their projects in clusters of three to five families.

5. Parent-Teen Seminars

Seminars where parents and teens learn together work well. We have done several of these at First Christian. One year, parents studied *Help, I'm the Parent of a Teenager* one night a week, while the teens studied the corresponding material in the manual at Bible school on Sundays. The parents and teens then met for one evening to talk about the material together.

6. Precious Metals Night

Silver and gold are considered precious metals. Those couples who have been married twenty-five years (silver) and fifty years (gold) have precious attitudes and insights that have enabled them to have long marriages. Designate a Sunday evening service as "Precious Metals Night" and interview several couples with long marriages. Use an informal talk show format and ask questions such as: "What is the secret of your long marriage?" and "What one thing would you like to pass on to the young couples of today?" Use this evening to honor all those who have had silver and golden wedding anniversaries. A small gift honoring these people would add interest to the evening.

Couples who have been married for many years have precious insights into successful marriages.

7. Family Night Emphasis

We recently used a Sunday evening service to encourage families to have regular family nights at home. We started the evening with a role play of a family having a disastrous family night and then one where the family used family night principles successfully. I followed this with some input about what makes a family night successful and Biblical precepts of teaching Christian values in the family (chapter six).

We then showed slides of families in our church having family nights. We ended the evening by showing family night resources including *Christian Family Activity* books and making these resources available to those who were interested.

8. Family Sermon Series

This may seem like a rather old idea but I have heard very few good sermons on the family. If a ministry to the family is going to be an important part of your church, the hows and whys of a strong family need to be talked about from the pulpit. Topics such as, "Foundations of a Christian Marriage," "Foundations of a Christian Family," "Teaching Christian Values in the Family," and "Biblical Principles on Communication," are just a few that could be dealt with in a sermon series.

9. Engaged Couples Interview

Set aside a service for engaged couples in your church. Raise the profile of your ministry to these couples by helping the church understand this ministry and how they can support couples through prayer.

How is God going to be a part of your marriage?

The service could be done like this: Interview the couples by asking such questions as, "Why are you choosing this time in your life to get married?" "Why did you choose this person?" "Why do you want to get married in the church?" and "How is God going to be a part of your marriage and family?"

This could be followed by a time of congregational prayer for these engaged couples' marriages. End your time together by going over your church's premarital policy and answering any questions people might have on your ministry to engaged couples.

10. Baby/Parent Dedication

A baby dedication day is a tradition with some churches. Here are some ideas to make this a more significant time for parents.

Call this event a baby and parent dedication. After all, it is the parents who are dedicating themselves to raising the child in the Lord. I was part of a baby and parent dedication service where the parents each made a statement of their spiritual goals for their baby, and their commitment to help that baby reach those goals. After each statement, there was a time of prayer for that child and his or her parents. I followed this with some remarks on the parents' Biblical responsibility to raise the child in the Lord.

11. Special Days

A good way to keep the importance of families in front of your congregation is to honor grandparents, mothers, and fathers on their special days. On Grandparent's Day (September of each year), we honor grandparents by presenting each of them with a carnation. We also give awards in special categories such as, "the grandparent who most recently went fishing with a grandchild," etc. Grandparents look forward to being honored each year. Mothers and fathers also look forward to being honored on their special days in similar ways.

12. Men's and Women's Seminars

I am very enthusiastic about seminars. We have found that men love to get together with men, and women love to get together with women for fellowship and learning. Here are several options for seminars:

(1) Have the seminar late on a Saturday afternoon (4:00 PM). Start with two, fifty-minute sessions, and then have a dinner or barbecue. Next, show a film that the group will enjoy. (For men, *A Father, A son, and A Three Mile Run* is a good choice.) Follow this film with discussion groups.

(2) Have an all-day seminar.

(3) Have a six-week seminar, meeting one evening each week. You can do this either in a large group setting or with small groups in homes. Two resources available from First Christian Church are *A Woman's Heart for God and A Man's Heart for God.*

(4) Have a speaker to address various men's or women's issues.

(5) Show a film or video series. Two I recommend are David C. Cook's *Famous Fathers Series* (includes leadership and participant materials); and *Maximum Marriage* from Tim Timmons, Box 2320, Newport Beach, CA 92660.

13. Christmas Project Night

A tradition here at First Christian is to devote the first Sunday evening of December to helping families prepare for the Christmas season. We started this tradition by having families and individuals make Advent wreaths. We provide the Styrofoam for the base, candles, greens, and a family night devotional guide to help make the lighting of the candles meaningful. Each year we add options. This year families can choose to make an Advent wreath, Advent calendar, dough ornaments, wooden Christmas tree ornaments, or Christmas placemats. A Christmas film is usually included in our evening service. This past Christmas we showed "Truce in the Forest," an outstanding Christian World War II film from Reader's Digest, based on a true life story.

14. Family-Related Bible-School Courses

A good way for your family ministry to reach people is through existing groups. Schedule periodic family courses in your adult Bible-school curriculum. The David C. Cook life-cycle curriculum is an example of a family course that could fit into an adult Bible school. Another I can recommend is *Understanding One Another,* a manual from our own Institute in Family Ministries here at First Christian in Napa. If some or all of your classes use electives, then scheduling a course on the family is a natural. Use the resources listed in this book as ideas for your curriculum. Check also with your Bible bookstore and publishers of Sunday-school materials for additional resources.

15. Family Retreats

Family retreats or camps are an excellent way for families to fellowship and learn together. During such a retreat, the purpose is for the *family unit* to spend time together. Schedule activities for the family designed to help them grow together. *Christian Family Activity Books* have activities that work well on retreats. After individual families have completed their activities, bring three to five families together to share what they have done.

16. Book Table

You may have noticed that your church library or media center is not the most visited spot in the building. Your family ministry committee can help to increase interest in reading, interest in self-improvement, and ultimately, interest in the church library, by having a periodic book table on Sundays. Make sure this table is in a well-traveled area. Offer some practical books on parenting, marriage, life-cycle issues, and personal growth. Have some of these for sale and some that people can borrow. You might also try maintaining a library bulletin board that each week features a book useful in strengthening marriages and families. A little write-up in the bulletin or a book report in the church paper can also stimulate interest in the material available in the church library.

17. Singles' Day

Singles often get lost in our churches. Especially in a family-oriented church, there is the danger of singles feeling out-of-place and overlooked. One of the many things you can do to counteract this problem is to have a Singles' Day. Have carnations for all singles (twenty-one and over perhaps). In the morning worship service, highlight some singles and their ministries. A sermon could be preached on singles such as, "Jesus was a Single Adult." Suggest that families in the congregation invite singles to their homes for lunch today and throughout the year. Remind them that singles often live away from their families and have no place to go for holidays. Encourage each family to "adopt" an older brother or sister.

Singles often get lost in our churches. Encourage each family to adopt an older brother or sister.

18. Old-Fashioned Sunday-School Picnic

Remember the old-fashioned Sunday-school picnics that you used to enjoy as a child? The entire church was there. You enjoyed sack races, lots of food, good fellowship, homemade ice cream, and so much fun. Isn't it sad that so few churches have these kinds of traditions anymore? The old-fashioned Sunday-school picnic was a way to bring the

the generations together. Why not have a picnic at your church this year? Make it potluck with the young and old urged to come. Have someone in charge of old-fashioned games such as sack races, three-legged races, wheelbarrow races, and plain old running races. Be sure and have people bring homemade ice cream.

19. Sunday-Evening Family and Personal Growth Instruction

The Sunday-evening service provides a good opportunity to give input on vital family and personal growth issues. Subjects such as guilt, grief, anger, self-talk, abortion, and suicide, can be covered by staff, lay people or professionals from your community.

DISCUSSION PROMPTER

Of the ideas represented, which three do you believe would work in your church and why?

9

LAUNCHING YOUR FAMILY MINISTRY

The success of your family ministry will depend on how well you assess needs, organize, plan, and carry out your plans.

In chapter two, "Planning Your Family Ministry," I gave a procedure patterned after Nehemiah that will help you develop a successful family ministry. The steps were as follows:

Personal Preparation
1. Pay Attention to the Facts
2. Respond to the Facts with Grief
3. Pray and Fast
4. Take Personal Responsibility

Proper Procedure
5. Ask Permission
6. Assess the Needs
7. Build a Team
8. Plan to Build
9. Overcome the Opposition

In this chapter we will pick up the "Proper Procedures" for launching your family ministry.

Follow Proper Procedures

In launching any kind of new ministry within the church, it is necessary to follow proper procedures. People often resist change, especially if it is an area they know little about or they see as some kind of threat. Nehemiah followed the proper procedures in launching his rebuilding effort.

5. Ask Permission (Nehemiah 2:1-9)

At the time Nehemiah wanted to go to Jerusalem to rebuild the wall, he was King Artaxerxes cupbearer. He asked the king for permission to rebuild the walls. He received the king's permission and support which helped Nehemiah launch his ministry of rebuilding. It will be important for you to share your vision with leadership and ask for permission to launch this ministry. If you are the minister of a church, you will need to share this vision with your elders and/or church board. If you are a lay person, you will need to share your vision with the minister and/or elders and ask permission to develop a ministry to families.

Whatever position you are in, I would suggest first reading this book and spending time in prayer. Next, observe the family and marriage needs in your church. Make a list of these needs. Create a vision for meeting the needs and then share the vision with the leadership. I am not suggesting that you present a full-blown program. Go with enough specifics, however, to give leadership a clear view of the potential of family ministries—enough facts to convince them and enough ideas to excite them.

A good way to get leadership excited about the possibility of solving a problem is to involve them in the process. Perhaps you could study this book together. The church staff, elders, or deacons could read the material privately and then discuss the questions together. This could be a part of monthly meetings or at a retreat. Whatever your approach, it is important to get others involved in the vision and decision.

6. Assess the Needs
(Nehemiah 2:11-15)

Once Nehemiah had permission to rebuild the wall, he assessed the needs. He inspected the entire wall in three nights to see what needed to be done. This is an important step for you to take in developing a family ministry for your congregation. You have seen needs in general, but now it is time to make a specific needs survey.

At First Christian in Napa, we do this every year. We believe it is important to keep current on what the greatest needs are. One way to find out is to ask. At the end of this chapter, there is a needs survey that we suggest you give to your church. Here are some guidelines for administrating the survey.

1) Give the survey at the morning worship service or Bible-school hour.

We administer ours during the Bible school.

2) Give the people time to fill out the survey and hand it in immediately. Do not let them take it home and bring it back later. People have good intentions but often fail to deliver.

3) Compute the results and make them available to the congregation.

4) Use the results as a guideline to establish goals (ministries) to meet the needs.

Accept Responsibility

7. Build a Team (Nehemiah 2:16-18)

After assessing the needs, Nehemiah started to gather his team so he could rebuild the walls. Nehemiah approached these people and said, "... 'You see the bad situation we are in, that Jerusalem is desolate and its gates burned by fire. Come, let us rebuild the wall of Jerusalem that we may no longer be a reproach'" (Nehemiah 2:17).

In order to build a family ministry in your church, you will need a team of people who share your vision for families and are willing to work at meeting their needs. Ideally, the entire leadership should share this vision, but the actual planning and implementing of family ministries will be through a team that you develop. I suggest that this be a Family Ministries Committee. In our church this is a standing committee but for some, it might need to start as a subcommittee of the Christian Education

Committee. The committee will need a budget of its own.

I recommend that you recruit four to six couples with an age range from twenties to fifties or sixties. Working with couples provides a good example of teamwork in marriages, and provides team leadership for implementing the various ministries. While we need the input of single parents, they will feel uncomfortable on a committee of mainly couples. To get the input from single parents, I meet with them separately.

Build a team of caring people who will commit themselves to strengthening marriages and families.

When recruiting committee members, look for couples who have a heart for the Lord, a commitment to the church, a commitment to growth in their own families, and a passion for helping other families. Do not try to persuade someone to be on the committee. Look for people who, when presented with the vision, will say, "Let us arise and build," like Nehemiah's team did (Nehemiah 2:18). Present the vision, and if they are the right people, they will respond with enthusiasm.

There are two ways to organize a Family Ministry Committee. One way is to use the Family Ministry Committee as a planning committee only. You assess the needs and plan ways of meeting those needs. With the planning committee only concept, members do not actually implement the plans. The committee delegates the actual ministries, such as marriage retreats, parental training, and communications seminars, to others who do the training.

A second way to organize is to have the Family Ministries Committee be both a planning and implementing committee. This the the way I prefer. The committee assesses needs and plans ministries to meet those needs, but is also involved in implementing the ministries. For example, in our church, the Family Ministry Committee couples are group leaders in our marriage enrichment classes, retreats, and parenting groups. This is not to say that they implement all ministries. We use other resource people both from inside and outside our church group. Since this type of committee plans and implements programs, it is important that part of your organizational meeting be for planning and another part for training. To begin with, you might want to study this book together chapter by chapter. See chapter for more discussion on training.

I like to use lay persons whenever possible in family ministry programing. We are plagued by the "expert syndrome" in our churches and especially in the area of family ministries. We believe that we must bring in an outside "expert" to speak on marriage, parenting, communication, self-esteem, grief, etc. While that is certainly an option, I believe that we miss the great potential of using "ordinary people" in our own congregations. If we base our program on outside experts, then family ministries will never penetrate the church. There should always be a good balance between "outside" and "inside" resources.

8. Plan to Build (Nehemiah 2:11-17)
Nehemiah assessed needs, built a team, and then devised a plan. He carefully divided the wall into sections and assigned responsibility for rebuilding those sections. Your family ministries team will need to plan to meet the needs you have discovered. Unlike a wall, however, family needs are vast, changing, and ongoing. You will not be able to plan to meet all needs. You will have to prioritize needs and meet the most important ones. For example, the first year you may be able to hold only one marriage retreat or one parent training group. It takes time to develop a family ministry. It is best to start small and develop gradually over a period of years.

In May or June of each year, we have a Family Ministry Planning Day. We take the entire day to plan our family ministries for the coming fiscal year (most of our ministries are from September through June). We first spend time with our needs assessment, prioritize needs, and then plan ministries to meet those needs. We meet monthly the rest of the year for continued planning of specific ministries and training. On the following page is an example of how we structure our planning day. Of course, you will want to make changes to reflect your viewpoint and needs.

Annual Family Ministries Planning Meeting

9:00—9:30—Devotional thought and prayer time

9:30—10:30—Discussion of the results of the needs survey. Prior to this meeting, each person should have read the results and formed some conclusion of his or her own.

10:30—10:45—Break

10:45—12:00—Now is the time to be specific about needs. On a large sheet of paper, chalkboard, or overhead projector, list the greatest areas of need. Next, prioritize those needs. Finally, decide on the needs that you will meet this year. Each person should have a copy of the work sheets on pages   . Use "planning worksheet one" for this project.

12:00—1:00—Lunch break

We usually have our planning days in a home and have pot-luck lunch.

1:00—4:00—Planning activities to meet the needs, setting calendar dates.

Now comes the hard work. You have decided what the family and relational needs are, now what can you do to meet those needs?

Use "planning worksheet two" to aid you in completing this task. List the need. Next, decide on a method for meeting the need. For example, if one of your high-priority needs is "better communication in marriage," what method will you use to meet this need? Will you want to hold a marriage retreat, have a film series or small, weekly marriage study groups, or another creative idea that your committee chooses? Who will be responsible for carrying out this plan? When will you hold this activity? You will need to calendar the event. Follow this procedure for each need you have decided to meet during the year.

When you have completed planning your year of family and relational events, use "planning sheet three" to list some needs you would like to meet in the next five years. When looking at year two, you can be fairly specific but years three, four, and five should be somewhat general. A needs survey each year will change some of your projected goals. Once you have planned your year, you will need to use your monthly meetings to carry out the plans.

9. Overcome Opposition
(Nehemiah 2:19, 10; 4; 6)

Nehemiah faced opposition to building the wall. He overcame the opposition and rebuilt the wall in fifty-two days. It took twelve years, however, to establish order in the people.

The lesson to us is this: There will be opposition to family ministries. Some people will not understand what you are trying to do. Others will be threatened by all the talk about relationships. Still others will say the church has no business teaching anything other than the Bible—no communication skills or other discovered truths. And we must

Satan does not want strong marriages and families. We can expect opposition.

also remember that Satan does not want strong marriages and families. He knows that strong marriages and families mean strong churches. We can expect opposition from the adversary.

You must be willing to take some abuse if you are going to be successful in family ministries. People resist change, and family ministries is going to bring about changes in individuals, couples, and families. You will become discouraged at times by the people who have needs but do not respond when programs are offered to meet those needs. Family ministries is exciting and rewarding but it is also hard work that takes diligence and patience. Are you ready for the challenge? It will take persons like you to help make our marriages and families glorfying to God and examples to the world.

Conclusion

God will bless your efforts as you minister in His name.

I am excited for you and your church. Family ministries will bring new excitement to the body as marriages, relationships, and families are strengthened.

Remember, it is better to start small—one or two activities for the first year—and then build year after year. God will bless your efforts as you minister in His name.

Family Life Questionnaire

We want to enrich the family and personal lives of persons in our church and community. To do this, we need to identify family and personal needs. By responding to the statements on this questionnaire, you can help us determine these needs.

We do *not* want names on these questionnaires. The results of your questionnaire will be combined with others to give us a comprehensive view of family and personal needs in our church.

In this questionnaire, you will find statements on various aspects of family and personal life. Read each statement and indicate the level of need you feel or your family's level of need. For example, if you feel that a statement only slightly represents a needy area in your family, circle number one or two. If the statement represents a very important need for you, then you would circle four or five. Indicate moderate levels of need by circling number 3. If the statement does not apply to you at all, circle 0.

Please give the following information:

Sex M   F
Age Category:
20-30   30-40   40-50   50-60   over 60
Marital Status:
Never married   married   divorced
separated   widowed

Information on Children

Sex	Age	Sex	Age
M F	____	M F	____
M F	____	M F	____
M F	____	M F	____

How many live at home?____ How many are adopted?____
How many stepchildren?____

Please rate the following family and personal needs:

Needed to Encourage a Vital Relationship With God

	Doesn't apply	low		med		high
1. Teaching that will help me apply Scripture to my daily life.	0	1	2	3	4	5
2. Teaching on doctrine	0	1	2	3	4	5
3. Increased knowledge of basics of Christian faith	0	1	2	3	4	5
4. How to establish an effective devotional life	0	1	2	3	4	5
5. How to deepen my prayer life	0	1	2	3	4	5

Needed to Strengthen Husband and Wife Relationships

6. How to have better communication in my marriage	0	1	2	3	4	5
7. How to ask for what I want and express how I feel without feeling guilty	0	1	2	3	4	5
8. How to work out appropriate husband and wife roles	0	1	2	3	4	5
9. How to have a better balance when making decisions	0	1	2	3	4	5
10. How to share openly with one another	0	1	2	3	4	5
11. How to handle conflict in a Christian manner	0	1	2	3	4	5
12. How to have a regular time of husband and wife devotions	0	1	2	3	4	5
13. Guidelines for sexual intimacy in marriage	0	1	2	3	4	5
14. How to set goals in marriage	0	1	2	3	4	5
15. How to restore romance in marriage	0	1	2	3	4	5
16. How to develop more things to do together	0	1	2	3	4	5

Needed to Build Family Strengths

17. How to effectively discipline my children   0 1 2 3 4 5
18. How to communicate better in the family   0 1 2 3 4 5
19. How to resolve differences in a Christian manner   0 1 2 3 4 5
20. How to instill a healthy self image in my children   0 1 2 3 4 5
21. Things to do, places to go as a family   0 1 2 3 4 5
22. How to be an effective single parent   0 1 2 3 4 5
23. How to handle issues with teenagers   0 1 2 3 4 5
24. How to deal with launching teenagers   0 1 2 3 4 5
25. How to have better in-law relations   0 1 2 3 4 5
26. How to build family togetherness   0 1 2 3 4 5
27. How to build a close personal relationship with my children   0 1 2 3 4 5
28. How to understand my role as a father/mother   0 1 2 3 4 5
29. How to teach my children to avoid sexual abuse   0 1 2 3 4 5
30. Understanding the developmental pattern of children   0 1 2 3 4 5

Needed to Enable Me to Teach Christian Values

31. How to teach Christian values to my children by my example   0 1 2 3 4 5
32. How to teach Christian values to my children in an informal way   0 1 2 3 4 5
33. How to have an effective family night   0 1 2 3 4 5
34. How to have regular family devotions   0 1 2 3 4 5

35. How to lead my child to Christ   0 1 2 3 4 5
36. How to teach Biblical moral values to my children   0 1 2 3 4 5
37. How to prepare my children for adolescence   0 1 2 3 4 5
38. How to prepare my children for dating, engagement and marriage   0 1 2 3 4 5
39. How to help my children be a success   0 1 2 3 4 5
40. How to talk to my children about sex   0 1 2 3 4 5
41. Resources for teaching Christian values to my children   0 1 2 3 4 5
42. How to communicate effectively with others   0 1 2 3 4 5
43. Knowing my personality style and how it fits with others   0 1 2 3 4 5
44. Establishing personal goals and a sense of direction   0 1 2 3 4 5
45. Help for overcoming self defeating behavior   0 1 2 3 4 5
46. Changing my view of myself   0 1 2 3 4 5
47. Coming to terms with my past   0 1 2 3 4 5
48. Overcoming depression   0 1 2 3 4 5
49. How to assert my rights without being aggressive or self-centered   0 1 2 3 4 5
50. How to handle anger   0 1 2 3 4 5
51. How to handle guilt   0 1 2 3 4 5
52. Overcoming fear and anxiety   0 1 2 3 4 5
53. Ability to be open with other persons   0 1 2 3 4 5
54. Programs, teaching and opportunities that focus on the single adult   0 1 2 3 4 5
55. Preparing for the retirement years   0 1 2 3 4 5
56. How to face personal crisis   0 1 2 3 4 5
57. How to deal with mid-life crisis   0 1 2 3 4 5
58. Controlling thoughts and managing emotions   0 1 2 3 4 5

59. How to manage finances	0	1	2	3	4	5
60. How to deal constructively with grief	0	1	2	3	4	5
61. How to deal with stress	0	1	2	3	4	5
62. How to forgive	0	1	2	3	4	5
63. Understanding suicide	0	1	2	3	4	5
64. Divorce recovery	0	1	2	3	4	5
65. How to arrange the priorities in my life	0	1	2	3	4	5
66. How to apply Biblical principles to my job	0	1	2	3	4	5
67. Managing A-type behavior	0	1	2	3	4	5

Please check any support group in which you would like to participate once a month;

_____ Divorce recovery
_____ Tough love (for parents with rebellious children)
_____ Marriage enrichment
_____ Never married
_____ Single again
_____ Stepparenting
_____ Young mother
_____ Marriage growth

What times are best for you to meet for marriage and family/personal enrichment?

_____ Sunday during Bible-school hour
_____ Week nights M T W TH F (circle one)
_____ Saturday morning/afternoon/evening (circle one)
_____ Sunday evenings

PLANNING WORKSHEET ONE

AREAS OF GREATEST NEED

_____

_____

_____

_____

PRIORITIZE NEEDS
   1.
   2.
   3.
   4.
   5.
   6.
   7.
   8.
   9.
  10.

NEEDS WE WILL MEET THIS YEAR

   1.

   2.

   3.

   4.

   5.

PLANNING WORKSHEET TWO

HOW WE WILL MEET THESE NEEDS

Need 1 - _____

    Method (Include how—seminar, retreat, etc., topic, resource, resource person and time slot— weekend, weekday etc.)

    Who
(will be responsible)_____

    When
(Calendar the event)_____

Need 2 - _____

    Method

    Who

    When

Need 3 - _____

    Method

    Who

    When

Need 4 - _____

    Method

    Who

    When

PLANNING WORKSHEET THREE
FIVE YEAR PLAN

YEAR ONE

YEAR TWO

YEAR THREE

YEAR FOUR

YEAR FIVE